THE WORLD'S RICHEST MAN

THE WORLD'S RICHEST MAN

Carlos Slim In His Own Words

EDITED BY TANNI HAAS

AN AGATE IMPRINT

CHICAGO

Printed in the United States.

Library of Congress Cataloging-in-Publication Data

Slim, Carlos, 1940-
 The world's richest man : Carlos Slim in his own words / edited by
Tanni Haas.
     pages cm
 Includes bibliographical references.
 ISBN 978-1-932841-84-8 (pbk.) -- ISBN 1-932841-84-9 (pbk.) -- ISBN
978-1-57284-734-7 (ebook) -- ISBN 1-57284-734-4 (ebook)
 1. Slim, Carlos, 1940---Quotations. 2. Businesspeople--Mexico--
Quotations. 3. Business--Quotations, maxims, etc. 4. Finance--
Quotations, maxims, etc. 5. Conduct of life--Quotations, maxims, etc.
I. Haas, Tanni. II. Title.
 HC132.5.S65A25 2014
 086.1--dc23

                              2014006037

10 9 8 7 6 5 4 3 2 1

B2 is an imprint of Agate Publishing. Agate books are available in bulk
at discount prices. For more information, go to agatepublishing.com.

In loving memory of my father, Jakob Haas

TABLE OF CONTENTS

INTRODUCTION

When Carlos Slim claimed the top spot on *Forbes*'s annual list of the world's richest people in 2010 (a position he maintained until 2013), it was the first time since 1994 that this top spot wasn't occupied by an American and, even more impressively, the first time ever that a person from a developing country had risen to number one.

Born in Mexico to parents of Lebanese descent, Slim, a civil engineer by training, owns or has significant stakes in more than 200 companies in various industries; however, the majority of his wealth, which is currently estimated at $72 billion, stems from his holdings in landline and mobile telecommunications. He's perhaps best known in the United States as being the largest shareholder in the New York Times Company, outside the Ochs-Sulzberger family, and for owning a major stake in Saks, Inc.

Slim, who began his investment career at age 12, has a lot in common with another of the world's richest people: Warren Buffett, of Berkshire Hathaway fame. Like Buffett, Slim has an uncanny ability to identify undervalued companies, build them up, and then sell them at a tremendous profit. He attributes that ability to the example of his father, himself a successful businessman, who taught Carlos to buy during times of economic crisis (when nobody else is buying).

Slim isn't only a talented businessman; he's also a major philanthropist. Believing that wealth is a responsibility rather than a privilege, he's donated billions of dollars through his various nonprofit foundations to education, health care, and job training for Latin America's poorest people. He's partnered with many other nonprofit organizations, including the Bill and Melinda Gates Foundation, the Clinton Global Initiative, and the Grameen Trust, and has received numerous awards and prizes for his philanthropic work.

Although Slim is fabulously wealthy, he lives a relatively modest life. Residing in the same house in Mexico City for the last 40 years, he wears inexpensive clothing from his Sears retail chain and drives himself to and from work (albeit with a security detail).

After undergoing open-heart surgery and losing his wife to kidney disease in the late 1990s, Slim began to transition the day-to-day responsibilities of his businesses to his three sons, Carlos Jr., Marco Antonio, and Patrick, while still staying involved with the strategic direction of his vast business empire and taking an active role in his nonprofit foundations. And, as the following pages show, Slim has much experience and sound advice to share about business, investing, leadership, and the economy, as well as his personal philosophies about work, wealth, and family, among many other topics.

BUSINESS AND INVESTMENT

. . . .

Go Beyond Your Home

You have to have an international reference of competition. You have to have the highest [standards].... Think of an athlete. He may be very good in his own house, but not as good as his neighbors. You have to go beyond your home. You have to go worldwide.

—No Fear of Failure: Real Stories of How Leaders Deal with Risk and Change, 2011

. . . .

Simplicity in Business

It's important to simplify...and take out everything that is secondary, to have less variables to study or to look at. Because when you have a lot of variables, and you don't make a distinction between the ones that are essential and the secondary ones...you have confusion.

—Academy of Achievement, December 2, 2007

● ●

The Benefit of Being Smaller

Small- and medium-sized enterprises generate greater and more diverse employment opportunities, economic activity, and human and business development.

—Clinton Foundation, June 17, 2010

● ●

Microsoft

Microsoft is one of the great companies of the 21st century.

—*Bloomberg Businessweek*, February 21, 2000

● ●

Focus on Operation

We focus on operation. We take down as many [management] levels as we can, to make the highest level be near the operation. With practice and experience, we make a team that's very efficient, and we do that very fast.

—Academy of Achievement, December 2, 2007

· ·

His Father's Business Ventures

My father always included us in his business ventures. From a very young age he talked with us about the problems within various enterprises and the solutions you could find by tackling the problem uniquely.

—*Carlos Slim: The Richest Man in the World*, 2013

· ·

The Power of Excess

One of the important lessons—especially from the Lehman crisis—is the power of excess. Periods of excess make you ambitious, but not always for the right thing.

—*Korn/Ferry Briefings on Talent & Leadership*,
Fall 2010

· ·

Learning from the Past

If you're in business, you need to understand the environment. You need to have a vision of the future, and for that you need to know the past. That is very important.

—Academy of Achievement, December 2, 2007

• •

Investing

Whomever doesn't invest for any reason, out of fear, precaution or whatever, will stay behind.

—*Agence France-Presse*, March 9, 2011

• •

Money That Leaves

Money that leaves the company evaporates.

—Carlosslim.com, 2007

• •

Reading a Company by the Numbers

The numbers tell you what is happening. You can read with the numbers. If things are going well, if things are not going well…. The numbers talk to you…. [Y]ou read the numbers and you understand what is happening in the companies.

—*Larry King Live*, December 3, 2010

• •

Risks

I never take risks. Maybe small risks, but I think I am not a risk taker. I think I am very conservative. All my life I have been very conservative.

—Academy of Achievement, December 2, 2007

• •

His Role in the Telecommunications Market

We want to be the smallest among the large companies on the market, with a globalized operation.

—*Gazeta Mercantil*, March 13, 2000

• •

Share Prices

The share price is important—in the end. But when does the end come? We take the long-term view.

—*Financial Times*, February 25, 2013

• •

Technology and Communications

Since the rise of man...about two and a half million years ago, all human societies and social changes have been driven by two fundamental factors: technology and communications.

—Keynote Address at the National Autonomous University of Mexico, June 21, 2010

• •

Telecommunications

Telecommunications is the nervous system of our civilization and as such it is a sector to be fostered.

—*El Financiero*, October 19, 2009

• •

The *New York Times*

I think it's a great newspaper, the best of the world. A great brand.

—CNBC, October 30, 2008

. . . .

The Content

We believe in [the *Times's*] media content. We think paper will disappear, but not the content. The content will be more important.

—*New Yorker*, June 1, 2009

. . . .

Alliances

In this new wave of technology, you can't do it all yourself, you have to form alliances.

—*Bloomberg Businessweek*, February 21, 2000

. . . .

Why His Company Is Bigger

If Walmart invests a billion dollars and others invest $100 million, Walmart is going to grow more. So if we invest $2 billion a year over many years and others invest $500 million or $100 million, it's illogical for them to have the same size as us.

—*Arizona Republic*, May 30, 2007

• •

They Will Run

In an acquisition, we don't really move people.
We cannot get involved at that level with so many
companies. Besides, if you move people, they
will run.

—Korn/Ferry Briefings on Talent & Leadership,
Fall 2010

• •

Interconnections

One company does not have to be all over the
world. We think more on the side of alliances and
interconnections and agreements instead of companies everywhere.

—Business Mexico, August 2002

• •

Business Decisions

When we decide to do something, we do it
quickly.

—Bloomberg Businessweek, March 28, 2005

● ●

His Business Goals

The goal is to make companies grow, develop, be competitive, be in different areas, be very efficient, to have a great human theme inside the companies.

—*Larry King Live*, December 3, 2010

● ●

Business Mortality

As much as infant mortality has decreased, let's reduce business mortality, especially for really small businesses. That can be achieved with less regulation or no regulation at all so that there are no impediments for them to develop and get the financial resources to operate.

—*Carlos Slim: The Richest Man in the World*, 2013

● ●

Acquisitions

Buying well is a discipline.

—*Arizona Republic*, May 30, 2007

• •

Understanding How to Solve Problems

I believe that the skills, the training, of the entrepreneur are very good to solve social and economic problems. Not because you have economic resources, or material resources, but because you know how to manage these resources. You understand how to solve problems.

—American Academy of Achievement,
December 2, 2007

• •

Competition

Competition makes you better, always, always makes you better, even if the competitor wins.

—Carlosslim.com, 2007

• •

Competition and Progress

If we don't compete with anyone, we'll never progress.

—*Carlos Slim: The Richest Man in the World*, 2013

• •

Internal Competition

[G]roups cannot compete against each other inside the company. We need to go in the same direction—not competing on the inside but competing on the outside.

—No Fear of Failure: Real Stories of How Leaders Deal with Risk and Change, 2011

• •

Competitiveness

Competitiveness is...a paradigm, and people need to be strong and know how to compete.

—American University of Beirut, March 18, 2010

• •

Executives versus Entrepreneurs

I always knew that I'm not an executive. I'm more an entrepreneur. I'm not a person that works from 8:00 to 6:00, or 9:00 to 5:00. I don't have the characteristics of the executives.

—Academy of Achievement, December 2, 2007

• •

They Will Have to Win It

We will not allow them to tie our hands in order
to steal our market. If they want it, they will have
to win it.

—*Inter Press Service*, February 10, 2000

• •

Open to Competition

We have never opposed the entry of a competitor.
Let them come on in.

—*New York Times*, June 28, 2007

• •

Fear of Competition

We aren't afraid of competing with anyone. What
we want is that they invest, that they don't take
advantage of our investments.

—*Yahoo! News*, February 1, 2012

• •

Getting into Crises

When there is a crisis, that's when some are inter-
ested in getting out and that's when we are inter-
ested in getting in.

—*Banderas News*, April 25, 2007

• •

Crises Are Temporary

We know that crises are always temporary and there is no evil that lasts 100 years, there is always an overshoot. When there is a crisis that provokes an adjustment, an overreaction comes along and things get undervalued.

—*Reuters*, March 10, 2010

• •

Opportunities

All crises are opportunities.

—*El País*, June 8, 2008

• •

Good or Bad Times

There are no good or bad times for the people that...have the means to work.

—CNN, November 14, 2011

· ·

Development for Business Reasons

There's no better investment than promoting [Latin America's] development. [US companies] shouldn't do it to be Good Samaritans, but for good business reasons. Imagine all the products they could sell for health, infrastructure, and education. And as they incorporate more people into the consumer culture, it will create more demand for their products.

—*Bloomberg Businessweek*, February 21, 2000

· ·

Dividends

When a company starts with a dividend policy, it is extremely negative for it to lower dividends or even to freeze them.

—Carlosslim.com, 2007

· ·

Economic Cycles

Economic cycles make sense in [an] agricultural civilization when you have good weather and bad weather. But in a society of services, it's a psychological problem, no?

—Academy of Achievement, December 2, 2007

• •

Globalization

Globalization has always been the result of communications.

—Carlosslim.com, 2007

• •

The Key Is the Internet

The key is the Internet…. The Internet is the heart of this new civilization, and telecommunications are the nervous system, or circulatory system.

—Bloomberg Businessweek, February 21, 2000

• •

In Bad Shape

In business, you invest when things are not in good shape. When you invest at these times, you take a better position than your competitors. When there is a recession and your competition does not invest, they are giving you the advantage.

—No Fear of Failure: Real Stories of How Leaders Deal with Risk and Change, 2011

Investment Philosophy

A businessman once asked me, "How do you decide on your investments? Is it the P.E. [price-to-earnings ratio] or the assets?" I said, "It's the potential for profit. I invest for the long term, not the short. If you buy something because it's cheap, that's only speculation."

—*New Yorker*, June 1, 2009

Investing Excessively

The one who sells and buys all day is like a gambler. He looks for the adrenaline [rush], like kind of a Rambo, an economic Rambo, a business Rambo, [a] financier Rambo.

—Academy of Achievement, December 2, 2007

Investing in Developed versus Emerging Markets

Whether one should invest more in developed or emerging markets is a sterile debate. What counts more is whether there are growth opportunities.

—*Financial Times*, June 12, 2011

• •

Investing in Mexico

Mexico has a healthy banking system, healthy macroeconomics, and a good labor pool—our people have proven they can work hard and efficiently in all sectors of the economy. So we have all the desired conditions to be a very attractive place for investments, both national and international.

—*Leaders*, October–December 2012

• •

Investing in Latin America

The fertile ground is Latin America...within 10 or 15 years, it is going to break the barrier of under-development and it is going to form a large middle class so we have to invest and invest heavily.

—*Financial Times*, June 12, 2011

• •

Clear, Attainable Targets

We avoid the trendy and the fashionable and concentrate on clear, attainable targets.

—*Institutional Investor*, June 1, 2003

•••

Investors versus Entrepreneurs

There is a difference between being an investor and being an entrepreneur. An entrepreneur actively creates and an investor passively invests.

—*Leaders*, October–December 2012

•••

US Investments in Mexico

The US investment in Mexico is not enough…. I think the US is being left behind. In Mexico, they are not in the banks; they are not in telecommunications, water or power. They are in traditional industries. They need to invest more in Mexico.

—*Korn/Ferry Briefings on Talent & Leadership*,
Fall 2010

•••

Avoid Large Mistakes

All businesses make mistakes. The trick is to avoid large ones.

—*Institutional Investor*, June 1, 2003

Old-Style Business

One of the big errors people are making right now is thinking that old-style businesses will be obsolete, when actually they will be an important part of this new civilization. Some retail groups are introducing e-commerce and think that the "bricks" are no longer useful. But they will continue to be important.

—*Bloomberg Businessweek*, February 21, 2000

How He Has Developed as a Businessman over Time

You develop a consciousness about your responsibilities and about the areas in which you must compromise. You look at things differently that you are working on. You develop international references regarding competition because you are competing internationally. You learn over time.

—*Korn/Ferry Briefings on Talent & Leadership*, Fall 2010

LEADERSHIP

. . . .

Giving People a Sense of Purpose

It's very important for leaders in business to work to create human capital that way, to give a sense of purpose to a team, and to the people in the organization. If leaders do this, then people working in organizations will feel they are doing something important for society and for the people around them. They will have a real sense of achievement.

—*Korn/Ferry Briefings on Talent & Leadership*,
Fall 2010

. . . .

Mistakes

If you don't make mistakes, it is because you don't make decisions.

—*El País*, June 8, 2008

• •

The Worst Mistake

Only the ones that don't make decisions, don't make mistakes. But the worst mistake is to not make a decision.

—WTTC Americas Summit, May 17, 2012

• •

Emotional Needs

I believe the leader sets the direction, and even the emotional tone, of an organization. It is about satisfying the emotional needs of people. It's not about taking responsibility for things.

—*Korn/Ferry Briefings on Talent & Leadership*, Fall 2010

• •

Developing Leaders from the Inside

The people that are inside the group follow our philosophy. We have a philosophy of leadership—some ideas and some concepts. They need to share this. Also, because they are inside the company, we see that they work together and not against each other. We all need to go in the same direction.

—*Korn/Ferry Briefings on Talent & Leadership*, Fall 2010

• •

Leadership Attributes

A true leader does require three scarce attributes: intelligence, courage and benevolence. Some leaders are brave and smart, yet bad-tempered and destructive; others are benevolent while lacking the two other attributes.

—Keynote Address at the First International Congress of Miraflores College, February 12, 2011

• •

Management Layers

It's not a question of arriving [at a new company] and putting in a whole new administration, but instead arriving and "compacting" things as much as possible, reducing management layers. We want as few management layers as possible, so that executives are very close to the operations. We also don't believe in having big corporate infrastructures.

—*Bloomberg Businessweek*, February 21, 2000

••

Organizational Culture

You need to have a culture that is flexible, and that people can adapt to, and that they feel they would like to join with pleasure.

—Korn/Ferry Briefings on Talent & Leadership,
Fall 2010

••

Teamwork

An investor, a speculator, can do it by himself. Well, nearly by himself. He needs information but he can do it without any people, with a small office. But if you're operating a business, if you're operating companies, if you're operating industries, you need a team to make it happen. Always look to make it better, and as long as you have a good team, you can do that.

—Academy of Achievement, December 2, 2007

••

Creating

The point is not to guard or conserve what you have, but to create. It's like planting a fruit tree.... You water it. You care for it so it grows.

—Korn/Ferry Briefings on Talent & Leadership,
Fall 2010

• •

Developing Human Capital

It's...what we do all the time in our companies. We are training people to be the best and to develop their know-how to learn.

—*Korn/Ferry Briefings on Talent & Leadership,*
Fall 2010

• •

Employees

People who work with us know that they can go as far as their talent will take them. We don't just care about doing the job. We also care about doing the job in the right way.

—*Korn/Ferry Briefings on Talent & Leadership,*
Fall 2010

• •

Achievements

People need to feel very good about their achievements. They get pride from what they are doing.

—*No Fear of Failure: Real Stories of How Leaders Deal with Risk and Change,* 2011

• •

Facing Our Problems

When we face our problems, they disappear. So learn from failure and let success be the silent incentive.

—American University of Beirut, March 18, 2010

• •

Founders versus CEOs

All companies start small and grow.... But as the businesses grow, sometimes the founder is no longer the best person to run the company. Then, you need to find the best people to run the business. You need to find the best executives—people who do that particular job very well. I say this because the CEO is very important to the success of the organization.

—*Korn/Ferry Briefings on Talent & Leadership*, Fall 2010

• •

How to Identify Great Leaders

The best way to find out is to look at what they have done in the past.

—*Korn/Ferry Briefings on Talent & Leadership*, Fall 2010

PERSONAL

· ·

Being Rich

It's not a football match you have to win or an Olympic event with a gold medal. It is not a contest or a competition.

—*Financial Times*, September 27, 2007

· ·

What Keeps Him Awake at Night

Jokingly:
Too much dinner…. But only when I have indigestion.

—CNN, November 14, 2011

· ·

Accept Them, Correct Them, and Forget Them

Mistakes are normal and human. Make them small, accept them, correct them, and forget them.

—American University of Beirut, March 18, 2010

• •

Optimism

Firm and patient optimism always yields its rewards.

—Carlosslim.com, 2007

• •

Pessimism

Chronic pessimism leads...to mediocrity.

—Commencement Speech at George Washington
University, May 19, 2012

• •

Money

Money does not motivate me. It is my view that when families have money in excess and they are not making investments and building businesses and creating jobs and doing things for society— when they think only materially—then something is wrong.

—*Korn/Ferry Briefings on Talent & Leadership*,
Fall 2010

• •

Negative Feelings and Emotions

Do not allow negative feelings and emotions to control your mind. Emotional harm does not come from others; it is conceived and developed within ourselves.

—Carlosslim.com, June 1994

• •

The Numbers

The numbers, they talk to me.

—*New Yorker*, June 1, 2009

• •

Words versus Numbers

I like numbers. Words speak to some people; to others of us it's numbers.

—*Arizona Republic*, May 30, 2007

•••

Time Management

I don't believe in working 20 hours or 16 hours or 14 hours. When you work too much, it is because your job is beyond you...because you're not organized. You don't have delegation of your responsibility, and I don't believe that in any business, in any activity, you need to work 15 or 16 hours, and...[not] have time for yourself or for your family or for anyone.

—Academy of Achievement, December 2, 2007

•••

Vocations

I think we all have vocations. There are some who are meant to be bullfighters, others are meant to be priests, doctors, and journalists. For me, since childhood, I liked investments.

—*Carlos Slim: The Richest Man in the World*, 2013

· ·

Wealth Distribution

I don't believe that you need to create wealth and then make a distribution plan for it. I think wealth is created because the market is growing and society is growing and then the overall economy grows. It's classical economics.

—*Korn/Ferry Briefings on Talent & Leadership*,
Fall 2010

· ·

Wealth Is Like an Orchard

Wealth is like an orchard. You have to share the fruit, not the trees.

—*Telegraph*, March 11, 2010

· ·

What It Means to Him to Be the Richest Person in the World

Nothing.

—*ABC News*, October 8, 2007

· ·

Water off a Duck's Back

Regarding his wealth:
It's water off a duck's back to me…. It doesn't matter.

—*BBC News,* August 7, 2007

· ·

Why He Doesn't Live in a Bigger House

What for? So that you can get lost in it? No, in my house I live with my children. It's a sociable space— one for sharing and meeting people in.

—*Financial Times,* September 27, 2007

· ·

Why He Won't Retire

You don't expect an artist to retire just because he's finished a certain number of paintings. It's their vocation, and for me work isn't only a social and business responsibility, it's also an emotional need.

—*Guardian,* July 6, 2007

• •

Words He Lives By

It sounds better in Spanish, but I'll say it in English anyway: "Impose your will against your weakness." That is what I believe.

—*Korn/Ferry Briefings on Talent & Leadership*,
Fall 2010

• •

Work

Work that's done well is not only a responsibility to one's self and to society, it is also an emotional need. You cannot live without doing something; [you need] a direction in life.

—*No Fear of Failure: Real Stories of How Leaders Deal with Risk and Change*, 2011

• •

Being Like Warren Buffett

I don't think I'm really like him. I think that I am more of an operator of companies than he is. I buy companies for strategic reasons and operate them.

—*Bloomberg Businessweek*, February 21, 2000

The New York Yankees

When asked whether he'd like to buy the team:
No. I like baseball to enjoy. If you're in business,
you are not enjoying. You are working.

—*Daily Beast*, September 27, 2011

Computers

My children gave me a laptop for Christmas, but
all I know how to do so far is push the "on" but-
ton. I also can turn it off. It's like learning chess
or golf, it takes a long time to learn some things.
The younger generation is much better at using
computers.

—*Bloomberg Businessweek*, February, 21, 2000

Paper Man

I'm a paper man, not electronic.

—*BBC News*, July 4, 2007

His Critics

If society were to tell me to get out of business, I would do it, but please ask my critics what they have done for the country. How many jobs have *they* created? Oh, how they hate me!

—*New Yorker*, June 1, 2009

Public Opinion

Sometimes when you are successful in business, you have others trying to turn public opinion against you because they are trying to compete with you.

—*Fortune*, August 20, 2007

Early Start

When I was very young, maybe 12 years, I began to make investments.

—*Larry King Live*, December 3, 2010

. . . .

Family Business

I don't consider this a family business. Our businesses are focused on the bottom line…. My relatives hold their jobs because they are good at them. If a relative wants to enter one of our businesses, he or she can get in easily enough, but any promotion will depend on merit.

—*Institutional Investor*, June 1, 2003

. . . .

Find the Job for Their Strengths

I think it's a bad decision to give a child a great job simply because he is your child, and I don't like it when someone places too much pressure or over-expects from them because they are your child. You must find the job that goes with their strength, their talents, their personality, pleasure and drive. Otherwise no one wins.

—*Carlos Slim: The Richest Man in the World*, 2013

. . . .

His Biggest Influence

My father.

—*Korn/Ferry Briefings on Talent & Leadership*,
Fall 2010

• •

Fear and Guilt

Live without fears and without guilt. Fear is the worst sentiment of human beings. It weakens us, inhibits actions, and depresses us. Guilt is a tremendous burden that weighs down our thinking, our actions, and our lives. Fear and guilt make the present difficult and obstruct the future.

—Commencement Speech at George Washington University, May 19, 2012

• •

Follow Your Conscience

Act always as your conscience dictates, because it never lies.

—Carlosslim.com, June 1994

• •

Fortitude and Emotional Balance

Fortitude and emotional balance are part of your inner self and are achieved by avoiding negative feelings such as envy, jealousy, arrogance, egoism, and greed, feelings that are a poison which is ingested bit by bit.

—Commencement Speech at George Washington University, May 19, 2012

••

Freedom

I believe in the freedom to create your own future.

—Academy of Achievement, December 2, 2007

••

Happiness

Real happiness...is a product of who you are and how you conduct yourself on a daily basis.

—Commencement Speech at George Washington University, May 19, 2012

••

Money Can't Buy Happiness

To think that happiness comes from buying things is crazy.

—*Larry King Live*, December 3, 2010

••

How He Spends His Time

I spend most of my time studying new technologies. My main task is to understand what's going on and try to see where we can fit in.

—*Bloomberg Businessweek*, February 21, 2000

Company Analysis

I analyze companies constantly.

—*Gazeta Mercantil*, November 23, 2004

His Job

My job is to think.

—*New Yorker*, June 1, 2009

How He Thinks of Himself

I think of myself as an entrepreneur. But an entrepreneur who needs to manage people.

—*Korn/Ferry Briefings on Talent & Leadership*,
Fall 2010

Work Is an Emotional Need

I think that work is not only a social responsibility, but it is an emotional need. You need to work. You need to do things. You need to be active. You cannot be lazy.

—Academy of Achievement, December 2, 2007

· ·

Work–Life Balance

You will have a better professional life with a good personal life and family life than if you don't have a good personal life and a family life.

—Academy of Achievement, December 2, 2007

· ·

Family Life Is Crucial

Family life is not only compatible with work, it is crucial for getting your own job done.

—Keynote Address at the First International Congress of Miraflores College, February 12, 2011

· ·

Worrying about Others' Opinions

When you live for others' opinions, you are dead. I don't want to live thinking about how I'll be remembered.

—*Forbes*, June 1, 2007

· ·

Needing Others to Say Good Things

When you need others to say good things about you, you will have a problem, because that has no end. If you need others to say, "Oh, that's great!" there is no limit.

—Academy of Achievement, December 2, 2007

· ·

One's Own Sense of Accomplishment

One should not seek exposure or applause for the things one does, but simply do them well for one's own sense of accomplishment.

—Reuters, March 9, 2011

· ·

Success

Success is not about doing things well or even very well, or being acknowledged by others. It is not an external opinion, but rather an internal status.

—Carlosslim.com, June 1994

Success Is Your Life

Success is not to make money or to have companies or to be an outstanding professional. The success is your life. The success is your family, your friends. In this way I think I have been very successful, because of my sisters, my brothers, and especially because of my family, my children, my wife, and my friends. I think that's really success.

—Academy of Achievement, December 2, 2007

How He'll Be Remembered

I don't concern myself with how I'll be remembered, or *if* I'll be remembered. My family and friends will remember me fondly.

—*Carlos Slim: The Richest Man in the World*, 2013

A Positive Influence

At the end we depart with nothing; we leave behind only our work, family and friends, and, perhaps, a positive influence which we have planted.

—Carlosslim.com, June 1994

● ●

Lessons From His Father

I learned from my father that you continue to invest and reinvest in your business—including during crises.

—No Fear of Failure: Real Stories of How Leaders Deal with Risk and Change, 2011

● ●

We Can Only Do Things While Alive

What I learned is to always bear in mind that we leave with nothing, that we can only do things while alive...and that we must be efficient, careful and responsible in the managing of our wealth to create more.

—Carlosslim.com, 2007

● ●

Living

Live the present fully and intentionally. Let the past not be a burden. May the future be an incentive. Live with a sense of urgency when you are creating, when you are innovating, when you are solving problems, when you are building.

—Commencement Speech at George Washington University, May 19, 2012

••

Leaving Better Children for His World

Many people want to leave a better world for their children. I'm trying to leave better children for my world.

—*Fortune*, August 20, 2007

••

Leaving Children a Commitment

When you leave your children a company, you are leaving them a big responsibility and a commitment. You don't want to leave them with money; you want to leave them with a commitment.

—*Banderas News*, April 25, 2007

• •

Leaving Children Money

I believe that when you leave them a company,
you leave them work, responsibility and commitment, and when you leave them money…100, 50,
30, or 20 million, you leave them that for them to
be bums…. When you have a company that you
have to manage, even if there is a CEO, it is a job, a
responsibility, an effort and commitment with the
company, with yourself and with the country to
generate wealth. The issue is not to have, I do not
know how much cash, to spend and just be idle all
year round, the rest of your life.

—Carlosslim.com, 2007

• •

His Legacy

Jokingly, on how he'd like to be remembered:
I think they must teach that question in school,
because they always ask me that.

—*Arizona Republic*, May 30, 2007

••

Learning From Personal Crises

Any personal crisis—you have to use it to get stronger.

—New Yorker, June 1, 2009

••

Life

Life's road is very long, but it is traveled fast.

—Carlosslim.com, June 1994

••

What's Worthwhile Has No Price

What is most worthwhile in life doesn't have a price. Love, friendship, nature, forms, colors, sounds, and the smells that we perceive with our senses, these feelings that are only appreciated when we're awake and open to enjoying life. To be born is a miracle. We should love life always, even during the worst of circumstances. It makes us stronger and develops a positive sense within us and with others.

—Commencement Speech at
George Washington University, May 19, 2012

Enjoy Life

Live...with intelligence, with soul and senses aware and on the alert; get to know their manifestations and train yourselves to appreciate and enjoy life.

—Carlosslim.com, June 1994

Living Modestly

My bachelor house was better than where I have lived for 40 years.

—*Forbes*, March 7, 2012

A Big Place

When you have a big place, you don't see your family.... You don't meet each other.

—*Larry King Live*, December 3, 2010

Luck

I don't believe too much in luck. I believe in circumstances. I believe in work.

—George Washington University Global Forum, October 29, 2010

••

Lying

Always act as you are, never lie.

— American University of Beirut, March 18, 2010

••

A Lie Repeated

A lie repeated many times begins to be believed.

—*Arizona Republic*, May 30, 2007

PHILANTHROPY AND EDUCATION

•••

His Philanthropic Efforts

I don't think it should be called philanthropic....
[What we're doing] is not philanthropy. It is social
investment.

—*Financial Times*, September 27, 2007

•••

We Don't Give Money

We don't give out money. What we try to do is
solve problems.

—Milken Institute Global Forum, April 29, 2013

•••

Not a Problem of Money

I'm not doing enough. Because, for me, doing
enough is not a problem of money. It is an issue of
how much I am or am not solving problems.

—*Forbes*, March 9, 2007

••

Philanthropy

I believe that philanthropy is about more than writing a check. It is about giving your time, knowledge, commitment, and dedication; Mother Teresa gave her life for others—people like that are the real philanthropists.

—*Leaders*, October–December 2012

••

To Do and to Solve

The issue is not to give, but rather to do and to solve.

—Carlosslim.com, 2007

••

Social Responsibility of Business Leaders

Just as I think it's important to run companies well, with a close eye to the bottom line, I think you have to use your entrepreneurial experience to make corporate philanthropy effective. I believe that if a businessman knows how to efficiently manage his business, he should be able to manage a foundation efficiently.

—*Bloomberg Businessweek*, February 21, 2000

• •

Wealth as a Social Responsibility

A businessman has to feel solidarity with the country he lives in. Wealth must be seen as a responsibility, not as a privilege. The responsibility is to create more wealth.

—*Highbeam*, September 7, 2005

• •

Produce Wealth for Society

I think it's a social responsibility to make wealth produce more wealth, for at the end of the day it will go to society.

—Academy of Achievement, December 2, 2007

• •

Warren Buffett's Philanthropic Efforts

Jokingly:
It's very interesting, because he leaves those who're running his affairs the responsibility of being very profitable. If they're inefficient, or don't get real-term returns, they're not going to be running anything.

—*Pittsburgh Post-Gazette*, March 14, 2007

• •

Bill Gates's Philanthropic Efforts

Jokingly:

I think that what Gates has done is good, and above all, because he said he would devote full time to this, and half time to Microsoft, which makes time-and-a-half.

—*Pittsburgh Post-Gazette*, March 14, 2007

• •

The Problem of Poverty

Gates has to study how he can [fight poverty] in the same way that Microsoft...succeeded in business, because charity has not solved the problem [of poverty].

—*BBC News*, March 10, 2010

• •

Funding Charities

It will be a big mistake that companies like Microsoft, Apple, the leaders of the world in technology, be sold by the founders to put the cash to fund charities.... They shouldn't. It is more important that they continue [to] manage the companies.

—*CNBC*, January 20, 2011

• •

Businesspeople as Social-Problem Solvers

The business community should get involved, not just in terms of monetary donations but with issue solutions. It's about thinking through problems and giving your time and your talent to finding solutions. I don't see it as a think tank, but rather like an action tank.

—*Leaders*, October–December 2012

• •

Our Knowledge and Experience

It's important that our talents and experience are utilized in addressing social problems because we have the training to work effectively with human and financial capital and to address complicated environments with different conditions. When we use our knowledge and experience to work on social problems, we can find solutions.

—*Leaders*, October–December 2012

· ·

Social Challenges

I am convinced, very convinced, that business experience can really help to address the social challenges…. It is exactly the same in business, you deal with similar characteristics in terms of decisions, teams, leadership, problems, limited resources, etc.

—*Financial Times*, September 27, 2007

· ·

His Challenge in Life

My challenge in life is not to just build a bigger business but also to help our country in terms of development.

—*Leaders*, October–December 2012

· ·

Working Together

We are…confident that there is no challenge we cannot meet if we work together, with clear objectives and knowing the tools we have at our disposal.

—Carlosslim.com, 2007

Charity

Trillions of dollars have been given to charity in the last 50 years. Trillions of dollars. Debt relief. Donations. And they don't solve anything.

—*Australian Financial Review*, September 30, 2010

Poverty

Charity doesn't solve poverty.

—George Washington University Global Forum, October 29, 2010

Digital University

Education now will come through technological means. You cannot make thousands of universities or hundreds of thousands of professors, but with technology and the Internet you can have great courses and make a digital university.

—*Daily Beast*, September 27, 2011

• •

Education

[W]e need to move from traditional methods to education of the 21st century using today's technology.

—*Leaders*, October–December, 2012

• •

Teach Creative Thinking

We need to teach [students] creative thinking and how to research. Because of technology, our capital and financial assets and access to markets, we do not have to sacrifice one generation for another like before.

—American University of Beirut, March 18, 2010

• •

Domestication

I believe that, sometimes, more than educating our children, we do something like domestication. "Don't do that. Go there. Put that there. Take that out." Like we're training them, without any common sense or rationality, without formation.

—Academy of Achievement, December 2, 2007

• •

Understanding the World

If you are talking about education at school, the marks you have—compared with the marks of others—are just qualifications. They aren't the same as your knowledge, your way of understanding the world.

—Korn/Ferry Briefings on Talent & Leadership,
Fall 2010

• •

Fighting Poverty

We have to declare war, but instead of a military war, a war against poverty.

—Carlosslim.com, 2007

• •

Poverty as an Obstacle

To fight poverty is an economic need. If you don't fight poverty, the country doesn't develop.

—Academy of Achievement, December 2, 2007

••••••••••••••••••••••••••••••••••••••

The Answer Is Jobs

A lot of people make money out of poverty—studies, conferences, NGOs—it's a massive business. The answer is jobs, jobs, jobs. Work is the only way to dignify the receiver. It meets an emotional need. And it encourages development.

—*Financial Times*, June 12, 2011

••••••••••••••••••••••••••••••••••••••

The Best Investment

[T]he best investment is to invest against poverty and create jobs. You have to incorporate people who are marginal and living in poverty and bring them into the modern economic market.

—*Euronews*, October 26, 2011

••••••••••••••••••••••••••••••••••••••

Fighting Poverty—but Not with Charity

What we need to do as businessmen is to help to solve the problems, the social problems. To fight poverty, but not by charity.

—*CNBC*, January 20, 2011

Support, Not Money

I am convinced that the private sector needs to give support, not money, because charity has not solved poverty in hundreds of years.

—*Forbes*, March 7, 2012

Doing Instead of Giving

It is not a question of giving but doing.

—*Reuters*, April 12, 2007

Santa Claus

Our concept is more to accomplish and solve things...than giving; that is, not going around like Santa Claus. Poverty isn't solved with donations.

—*Pittsburgh Post-Gazette*, March 14, 2007

••

Fighting Poverty through Partnerships

The government and private sector combined
are very important to provide modern and high-
quality health and education to fight poverty and
all its consequences.

—*No Fear of Failure: Real Stories of How Leaders*
Deal with Risk and Change, 2011

••

Fighting Poverty with Education and Jobs

Poverty is resolved with education and jobs. You
don't need to teach a man how to fish, as the
Chinese used to say. Instead of giving him the
fish, instead of teaching him how to fish, you have
to teach him how to sell the fish so that he eats
something else besides a fish.

—*New York Times*, June 28, 2007

••

Dignity

Employment is the way to fight poverty and dignify a human being.

—Clinton Foundation, June 17, 2010

Improving the Economy via Education and Training

We need to help people out of poverty, train and educate them and put them in the labor market, and they will improve the economy and society.

—*Leaders*, October–December 2012

Giving and Receiving

When you give, do not expect to receive.

—Carlosslim.com, June 1994

Universal Access to the Internet

I think the Internet has a big potential worldwide. It's the nervous system of the new society, and it's very important in this society of knowledge and information and technology to have universal access to these services.

—*CNBC News*, November 16, 2009

POLITICS AND ECONOMICS

．．．．．．．．．．．．．．．．．．．．．．．．．．．．．．．．．

Businesspeople versus Politicians

I think that businessmen and entrepreneurs have more experience managing resources, and we can more easily solve the problems than politicians, who have other views. They are thinking about elections, they are thinking about popularity. I don't think that giving money should be something done for personal popularity.

—*Forbes,* March 7, 2012

．．．．．．．．．．．．．．．．．．．．．．．．．．．．．．．．．

$1

A businessman can do with $1 what a politician can do with $2, or many.

—Milken Institute Global Forum, April 29, 2013

••

Democracy

Democracy does not guarantee a good government, and it is not an economic model. It only guarantees that if we do not like the person governing us, when his period is over, we change him.

—Carlosslim.com, 2007

••

Economic Recovery

The important recovery is in the real economy. When employment begins to grow and sustain good figures, we will see a better time.

—*Bloomberg*, November 17, 2009

••

Economic Stability

Economic stability is a policy instrument, not an objective.

—*Free Republic*, September 7, 2005

● ●

Public and Private Investment

You need the combination of private investment and public investment, because public investment is not enough to solve the problems, and the innovation that people with business experience can bring is very important to solve these kinds of problems.

—Academy of Achievement, December 2, 2007

● ●

Free Trade

I believe free trade is important, because to trade is to negotiate with the other country.... Conditions that are convenient to both parties are negotiated, not that are convenient for one and not for the other, and negotiations have to be acceptable to both parties.

—Carlosslim.com, 2007

● ●

Immigrants

I think immigrants in general are very, very hard workers and very strong.... I admire immigrants from anywhere.

—Academy of Achievement, December 2, 2007

••

Mexico's Drug War

You [the United States] stay with the money and the drugs. We [Mexico] stay with the weapons and the violence. And you're selling the weapons to the consumers in Mexico. And the retail price [of the drugs] is, I don't know how much bigger, let's say 10 times in the U.S. what it is in Mexico. And that means the demand is here and the money is here. It's like what used to happen during Prohibition in Chicago. You had a lot of violence there.

—*Daily Beast*, September 27, 2011

••

Mexico's Federal Competition Commission

They won't let us do anything. They won't let us buy and they won't let us sell.

—*Latin Trade*, November, 2002

••

Political Ambitions

I have no political vocation. I prefer to work from the entrepreneurial and foundations world to form more and better human and physical capital.

—Carlosslim.com, 2007

• •

Political Leanings

I think a business man must stick to his business and his community, and stay away from political interests, projects, and agendas. I'm not a member of any political party nor do I ever care to become one.

—*Carlos Slim: The Richest Man in the World*, 2013

• •

Political Leaders

The solutions that [political leaders] are looking at are not the right solutions. They are not looking for a different way to solve the problem [of poverty].

—*Forbes*, March 7, 2012

• •

President Obama's Buffett Rule

I don't know what Warren Buffett pays, but I think that the fiscal policy should be fair. You don't need to raise taxes on rich people, because they create capitalization and investment. But you need to tax speculation—meaning capital gains. Why should it be just 15 percent? Salaried people pay 35 percent. Why shouldn't that be paid on capital gains?

—*Daily Beast*, September 27, 2011

• •

Pride

Pride is individual, internal; it is not about recognition or applause from others. It is the internal feeling you have for the things you do.

—*El País*, June 8, 2008

• •

Prosperity

In my view, prosperity is good. But if only one country is prosperous, it's still a small market. What do you do with all of the raw materials and production potential[?]... All of the labor? The more prosperity we have, and the more wealth we create, the better it is for everyone.

—*Korn/Ferry Briefings on Talent & Leadership*,
Fall 2010

• •

His Relationship with Government Officials in Latin America

It's always been said that we're competitors, but I think that we're very complementary.

—*Wall Street Journal*, October 8, 2003

• •

Known by the Public

In [a] democracy you need education; the thoughts of those in power have to be known by the public.

—Carlosslim.com, 2007

• •

Retirement Age

The excess of the welfare state in developed countries is in being burdened with the offer of early retirement…. Before, it was a society based on physical work, so you had to retire young. Today, we are a knowledge-based society, and people are retiring when they are in their best mental state, when they are most experienced, most trained. This is when the state most needs them.

—*Telegraph*, February 19, 2011

• •

Company Size

Small and medium enterprises play a key role globally as drivers of economic growth and job creation.

—*All Africa*, April 3, 2012

••

Where the Employment Is

The focus should be the support of small-
and middle-size business. That is where the
employment is.

—*Daily Beast*, September 27, 2011

••

Solving the European Economic Crisis

What Europe should do is sell assets…. Sell assets,
to reduce debt and deficits, but also invite the private sector…to make the investments the state no
longer has any business doing…. Motorways, even
hospitals and schools, can all be financed with
private money.

—*Guardian*, October 17, 2012

• •

Adjustments to the Welfare State

Regarding the European economic crisis:

The main reason for what is happening now [in Europe] is that, after World War II, governments established an increasingly larger welfare state that has become unsustainable. It is necessary to make some adjustments to this welfare state. They need structural changes, but you can see that these are not being undertaken, and that instead [governments] are resorting to the traditional recipe of adjusting the fiscal deficit through higher taxes or lower public spending.

—*El País*, October 21, 2012

• •

Europe's Assets

They have 10,000 kilometers of highways—they should collect a toll. They have airports—they should sell them. They have a great amount of assets that could be operated by the private sector.

—*Mexico Today*, May 30, 2012

Solving the US Economic Crisis

Aside from lowering taxes, we should be directing more money to the real economy, not to the financial economy. The volatility of the markets is so great that more is won or lost in a single day than in five years of accumulated interest. And that's not a good thing.

—*Daily Beast*, September 27, 2011

The Public Sector

Instead of stopping the investment in the public sector and creating austerity programs, which creates unemployment, it's better to rely on a development program financed by the private sector.

—*Wall Street Journal*, October 25, 2011

Modern Marshall Plan

For its own economic interest, the US should come up with a kind of modern Marshall Plan, incorporating the World Bank, the Inter-American Development Bank, and private companies.

—*Bloomberg Businessweek*, February 21, 2000

• •

Support the System

You need to support, not a company, not the
stockholders, but the system to avoid a systemic
problem.

—*CNBC News*, October 30, 2008

• •

Developing Latin America

I would hope that by 2015 Mexico and other Latin
American countries will have broken the barrier
of underdevelopment. You break that barrier by
having enough force to pull away from the gravi-
tational force that pulls you back. I believe you
can break that barrier once the per-capita income
is more than $10,000 or $12,000.

—*Financial Times*, September 27, 2007

MILESTONES

1940

Slim is born on January 28, 1940, in Mexico City, the fifth of six children. His father, Julián Slim Haddad, is a Lebanese-born businessman who came to Mexico at the age of 14, in 1902, to avoid being conscripted into the Ottoman army. Four of Julián's older brothers were already living in Mexico at the time of his arrival. His mother, Linda Helú, is a Mexican-born homemaker, herself the daughter of Lebanese immigrants. Both are of Catholic descent. Her father, José Helú, brought the first Arabic printing press to Mexico and founded one of the first Arabic-language magazines in Mexico.

1949

When Slim is nine, his father, the owner of a dry goods store called La Estrella del Oriente (The Eastern Star), pays him to go around town and compare competitors' prices to those in La Estrella.

1952

At age 12, Slim puts his savings in a checking account but, unhappy with the low return on investment, decides to buy government savings bonds instead.

1953

Slim's father passes away.

1961

Slim completes his bachelor's degree in civil engineering at the National Autonomous University in Mexico City, while supporting himself by teaching undergraduate courses in algebra and linear programming to his fellow students.

1965

Slim incorporates his first company, Inversora Bursátil (stock brokerage), acquires Jarritos del Sur (bottling), and establishes several other companies, including Bienes Raíces Mexicanos (real estate), Constructora Carso (construction), and Mina de Agregados Petreos el Volcán (mining).

1966

Slim marries Soumaya Domit Gemayel, with whom he later has six children: three sons (Carlos Jr., Marco Antonio, and Patrick) and three daughters (Johanna, Soumaya, and Vanessa).

Slim incorporates Inmobiliaria Carso (real estate).

1967

Slim establishes two companies: GM Maquinaria (construction equipment) and Promotora del Hogar (real estate).

1968

Slim acquires another company: Mina el Volcán SSG Inmobiliaria (mining).

1969

Slim establishes three additional companies: Bienes Raíces Mexicanos (real estate), Invest Mentor Mexicana (brokerage), and Nacional de Arrendamientos (real estate).

1972

At age 32, Slim has already established or acquired eight companies in construction, mining, and real estate.

1976

Slim acquires a controlling interest in Galas de México (printer of calendars and labels).

1980

Slim incorporates Grupo Galas (subsequently renamed Grupo Carso), combining all of his business interests.

1981

Slim acquires a controlling interest in Cigatam, Mexico's second-largest tobacco company and the producer of Marlboro cigarettes in Mexico.

1982

Slim makes a number of acquisitions, including a tire company (General Tire), an aluminum producer (Reynolds Aluminio), and a retail chain (Sanborns).
Slim acquires Mexico's largest insurance company, Seguros de Mexico.

1984

Slim's mother passes away.

Slim creates Grupo Financiero Inbursa (insurance) by merging Casa de Bolsa Inversora Bursatil, Fianzas La Guardiana, and Seguros de Mexico.

Slim acquires significant stakes in Anderson Clayton (cotton equipment) and British American Tobacco. He also acquires another tire company, Hulera el Centenario Firestone.

1985

Slim acquires a controlling interest in Artes Gráficas Unidas (packaging), Papel Loreto y Peña Pobre (paper mills), General Popo (tires), Hershey's (confectionary), and increases his shares in Reynolds Aluminio and Sanborns.

Slim is awarded the Medal of Honor by Mexico City's Chamber of Commerce for his business achievements.

1986

Slim acquires Minera Frisco and Empresas Nacobre (mining companies), Química Fluor (chemicals), and a controlling interest in Euzkadi (tires).

Slim establishes Fundación Carlos Slim (Carlos Slim Foundation), a nonprofit foundation that supports artistic and cultural activities (libraries, museums), education (computer equipment, student scholarships), and health care (hospitals, orphanages).

1990

Together with France Telecom and Southwestern Bell, Slim acquires the landline telephone company Telmex from the Mexican government for $1.7 billion. He's awarded the sole national cell phone license, which he will later use (in 2001) to establish América Móvil. He commits to investing $10 billion to modernize Telmex in exchange for a guarantee that he's protected from a hostile takeover. (Telmex, which as of 2013 had 80 percent of the landline market in Mexico, also operates in more than half a dozen other countries, including Argentina, Brazil, Chile, Colombia, Ecuador, and Peru.)

Slim acquires Radiomovil Dipsa (mobile telecom) and renames it Telcel.

1991

Slim acquires Hoteles Calinda (hotel chain), which is subsequently renamed OSTAR Grupo Hotelero.

1992

Slim acquires Condumex (auto parts).

1993

Slim increases his stakes in General Tire and Reynolds Aluminio, gaining majority interest in both companies.

1994

With financial support from the Carlos Slim Foundation, Slim establishes Museo Soumaya in Mexico City, an art museum named after his wife and designed by his son-in-law, Fernando Romero, which houses the world's second-largest (and largest private) collection of Rodin sculptures, including The Kiss. Museo Soumaya holds more than 70,000 works of art, including works by Dalí, Da Vinci, Picasso, Renoir, Rivera, and Toulouse-Lautrec. The museum also funds art research, conservation activities, and sponsors traveling art exhibitions.

Slim receives the Golden Plate Award from the American Academy of Achievement for his business achievements.

1995

Slim establishes Fundación Telmex (Telmex Foundation), a nonprofit foundation that, in addition to the areas covered by the Carlos Slim Foundation, also supports sports programs. Its most prominent activity is Copa Telmex, the largest amateur sports tournament in the world.

1996

Slim splits Grupo Carso into three companies: Carso Global Telecom, Grupo Carso, and Invercorporación.

Slim acquires a stake in US Internet services provider Prodigy Communications.

1997

Slim undergoes successful open-heart surgery.

Slim acquires the Mexican arm of Sears Roebuck and a smaller stake in Apple Computers.

1998

Following his open-heart surgery, Slim begins to hand over the day-to-day responsibilities of his businesses to his three sons, Carlos Jr., Marco Antonio, and Patrick, while staying involved with the strategic direction of his vast business empire and taking an active role in his nonprofit foundations.

Slim increases his stake in Prodigy Communications.

1999

Slim's wife dies of kidney disease.

Slim establishes a new company, Carso Infraestructura y Construcción, by merging Grupo Carso's construction and infrastructure divisions.

Slim acquires Pastelería Francesa El Globo (food).

Slim expands his telecommunications interests beyond Latin America by acquiring a stake in US cellular company Tracfone.

2000

Together with Microsoft, Slim launches a Spanish-language Internet portal called T1msn (subsequently renamed Prodigy MSN), which soon becomes the leading Internet portal in Mexico.

Slim acquires stakes in several Latin American cellular telephone companies, including ATL and Telecom Americas (Brazil), Techtel (Argentina), and Tricom (Dominican Republic).

Slim acquires stakes in OfficeMax, Philip Morris Companies, and Saks, Inc. He also acquires Guatemalan telecommunications company Telgua, and he sets up Telmex USA.

Slim establishes Fundación del Centro Histórico de la Ciudad de México (Mexico City's Historic Downtown Foundation) with support from the Telmex Foundation. The foundation works to restore and revitalize Mexico City's historic downtown area. Slim has been Chairman of the Executive Committee for the Restoration of the Historic Center since 2001.

2001

Slim spins off América Móvil (cellular telecom) from
Telmex. It eventually becomes Latin America's larg-
est cellular telephone company, with 70 percent of the
Mexican cell phone market. It operates in more than
a dozen countries, including Argentina, Brazil, Chile,
Colombia, Dominican Republic, Ecuador, El Salvador,
Guatemala, Honduras, Nicaragua, Panama, Paraguay,
Peru, Puerto Rico, and Uruguay.

Slim increases his stake in Saks, Inc.

Slim continues to acquire stakes in several cellular telephone companies in Brazil, including Americel, Telet,
and Tess, as well as a larger share of ATL.

2002

Slim acquires a controlling interest in two Latin American cellular telephone companies: Comcel (Columbia)
and Techtel (Argentina).

Slim is bestowed the decoration of Commander in the
Belgian Order of Leopold II by the Belgian government.

2003

Slim expands his Latin American operations by acquiring
stakes in several cellular telephone companies, including BSE and BCP (Brazil), Celcaribe (Columbia), CTE
(El Salvador), CTI (Argentina), and by increasing his
share in Conecel (Ecuador).

Slim establishes a nonprofit real estate company to help
with the restoration and revitalization of Mexico City's
historic downtown area.

Slim is named Industrialist of the Year by *Latin Trade*
magazine.

2004

Slim acquires several Latin American telecommunications companies, including Chilesat (Chile), Embratel Participações and Net Serviços de Comunicação (Brazil), Empresa Nicaragüense de Telecomunicaciones and Nicaraguan Entel (Nicaragua), and Megatel (Honduras), as well as increases his shares in CTE (El Salvador) and Techtel (Argentina).

Slim acquires AT&T Latin America (subsequently renamed Telmex Latinoamerica), with operations in Argentina, Brazil, Chile, Colombia, and Peru.

Slim receives the Fashion Group International Prize, the Hadrian Award (from the World Monuments Fund), and the Real Estate Developers Association Award for his efforts to restore and revitalize Mexico City's historic downtown area.

Slim is named Industrialist of the Decade by *Latin Trade* magazine.

Slim receives the Alliance Award from the Free Trade Alliance for his business accomplishments.

2005

Slim acquires the Chilean telecommunications company Smartcom.

With an initial investment of $800 million, Slim establishes Impulsora del Desarrollo y el Empleo en América Latina (IDEAL; in English, Driving Development and Employment in Latin America), a nonprofit construction-financing company that supports infrastructure development. It helps underwrite electronic toll collection systems, highways, offshore oil plants, ports, and water treatment plants, among other projects.

Slim receives the Galardón del Salón del Empresario
Award from Impulsa, a nonprofit foundation, for his
contributions to business and community development in Mexico.

The Telmex Foundation is named Foundation of the
Year by the Mexico City Chapter of the Association of
Fundraising Professionals, in recognition of its phil-
anthropic work.

2006

Slim acquires stakes in Verizon Dominicana (Dominican
Republic), Telecomunicaciones de Puerto Rico, and
Compañía Anónima Nacional Teléfonos de Venezuela,
all of which are part of United States–based Verizon
Communications. He also purchases a smaller share
in Univisión, a Latin American broadcasting company.

Slim receives the Lifetime Achievement Award from the
Worldwide Association of Mexicans Abroad.

2007

Slim acquires Ecuadorian telecommunications company
Ecutel.

Slim establishes the Carlos Slim Health Institute to
serve Latin America's poorest people.

The Telmex Foundation receives the National Sports
Award for its support of sports in Mexico. The award
is presented by President Felipe Calderón.

Copa Telmex, the amateur sports tournament sponsored
by the Telmex Foundation, is recognized by the *Guin-
ness Book of World Records* as the largest amateur
sports tournament in the world.

Slim is named Industrialist of Year by the Mexican
Foundation for Health.

2008

Slim acquires a stake in Citigroup and increases his stake in Saks, Inc.

Slim acquires a stake in The New York Times Company and a smaller stake in Independent News & Media, the publisher of the British newspaper the *Independent*.

Together with the Grameen Trust, Slim establishes a $45 million microfinancing program, which offers micro loans to the poorest people in Mexico.

Slim is appointed to the Executive Board of the RAND Corporation, a United States–based nonprofit research organization.

Slim is awarded the National Order of the Cedar by the Mexican Embassy of Lebanon for his philanthropic activities.

2009

Slim increases his stake in The New York Times Company and loans the company $250 million.

Slim establishes yet another nonprofit foundation, the Inbursa Foundation, to complement the work of the Carlos Slim Foundation and the Telmex Foundation.

The Carlos Slim Foundation, in partnership with the World Wildlife Fund, makes an initial investment of $100 million to support biodiversity and sustainable development in Mexico.

Slim receives the President's Medal from George Washington University and the ESADE Award, administered by Ramon Llull University in Spain, for his business and philanthropic activities.

Slim is named Man of the Year by the World Boxing
Council for his support of amateur and professional
boxing.

2010

Forbes reports that Slim is the world's richest person,
with an estimated fortune of $53.5 billion. Bill Gates
and Warren Buffett come in second and third, with
an estimated net worth of $53 billion and $47 billion,
respectively. It's the first time in 16 years that the
world's richest person isn't from the United States,
and the first time ever that that person hails from a
developing country.

The Carlos Slim Health Institute launches a $65 million
initiative to research the genetic origins of cancer,
diabetes, and kidney disease. It also partners with
George Washington University on an antipoverty
vaccine development project to fight neglected tropi-
cal diseases in Latin America.

Slim signs a contract to build the Atotonilco Wastewater
Treatment Plant, one of the biggest hydraulic infra-
structure works in Mexico, in partnership with the
National Water Commission.

Together with the Clinton Global Initiative, Slim establishes a $20 million fund to offer loans to small- and
medium-sized companies in Haiti suffering from the
effects of the January earthquake.

The Carlos Slim Foundation launches the Mesoamerica
Health 2015 Initiative together, with the Bill and
Melinda Gates Foundation, the government of Spain,
and the International Development Bank. The goal
is to reduce the gap in health care experienced by
the poorest 20 percent of the population in Southern
Mexico and Central America.

The International Telecommunications Union and UNESCO establish the International Broadband Commission for Digital Development to be chaired by Slim.

Slim is awarded the WBC Humanitarian Prize of the Year by the World Boxing Council for his support of amateur and professional boxing.

Slim receives the Lebanese Gold Order of Merit for his business achievements, presented by Michel Sleiman, president of Lebanon.

2011

Slim continues to top the *Forbes* list of the world's richest people, with an estimated fortune of $74 billion. Bill Gates and Warren Buffett come in second and third, with an estimated net worth of $56 billion and $50 billion, respectively.

Slim acquires a controlling interest in Colombian oil company Tabasco, and a smaller stake in Spanish-language media conglomerate Grupo Prisa.

Slim increases his stake in The New York Times Company and Saks, Inc.

Slim is included in *Forbes*'s list of the World's Biggest Givers, having donated more than $4 billion to philanthropy through his various foundations.

The Carlos Slim Foundation joins the global RED initiative to help fight the worldwide prevalence of HIV/AIDS.

Slim is awarded the Franco-Mexican Friendship Prize by the Franco-Mexican Chamber of Commerce and Industry.

Slim receives the Sor Juana Inés de la Cruz Medal by
Claustro de Sor Juana University in Mexico for his efforts to restore and revitalize Mexico City's historic
downtown area.

Slim is awarded the Quién 50 prize by *Quién* magazine
for being one of the most influential people in Mexico.

Slim receives the Sorolla Medal from the Hispanic Society of America for his support of arts and culture.

2012

Forbes names Slim as the world's richest person for the
third year in a row, with an estimated fortune of $69
billion. Bill Gates and Warren Buffett come in second
and third, with an estimated net worth of $61 billion
and $44 billion, respectively.

Slim acquires US mobile telephone company Simple Mobile (part of T-Mobile USA), as well as smaller stakes
in Royal KPN (the Netherlands), Telekom Austria, and
oil and gas producer YPF (Argentina).

Slim launches Ora.Tv, a digital television network, on
which his close friend, former CNN broadcaster Larry
King, hosts his own show, *Larry King Now*.

Slim becomes the first businessperson to host the presti-
gious Montevideo Circle in Mexico City, a forum for
presidents, diplomats, and businesspeople.

The Carlos Slim Foundation donates $3 million to expand
broadband services for Latin American families residing in the United States.

The Telmex Foundation receives the Socially Responsible
Enterprise Award from the Mexican Center for Philanthropy for its support of Mexico's social development.

Slim receives the Gibran National Committee Award for his contribution to spreading knowledge of the poet, philosopher, and painter Gibran Khalil Gibran.

Slim is awarded an honorary doctorate from George Washington University for his philanthropic activities and contributions to business and community development in Mexico and Latin America.

Slim receives the Leadership in Philanthropy Award from the Clinton Global Initiative.

Slim is awarded the Paz y Democracia prize by the José Pagés Llergo Foundation for his contributions to sustainable development.

Slim receives the Honor and Merit Badge from the International Red Cross for his philanthropic activities.

Slim is awarded the Dwight D. Eisenhower Global Leadership Award by the Business Council for International Understanding for his contributions to global commerce.

2013

For the fourth year in a row, *Forbes* names Slim the richest person in the world, with an estimated fortune of $73 billion. Bill Gates and Amancio Ortega come in second and third, with an estimated net worth of $67 billion and $57 billion, respectively.

Slim acquires a stake in CaixaBank, Spain's third-largest bank.

América Móvil is awarded the rights to broadcast the 2014 and 2016 Olympic Games on media platforms across Latin America. The company also invests $60 million in Mobli, an Israeli mobil media sharing platform; and $40 million in Shazam, a British company that makes the music recognition app of the same name.

Together with the Khan Academy, the Carlos Slim Foundation launches a $317 million program to support Mexico's educational system through increased access to online courses, digital libraries, and school equipment.

The Carlos Slim Foundation announces that it plans to donate $100 million to the Global Polio Eradication Initiative. The Foundation also donates $74 million to help with identifying disease-causing genes, in a collaborative research initiative with The Carlos Slim Health Institute, the National Institute of Genomic Medicine, and the Broad Institute of MIT and Harvard.

Together with the Bill and Melinda Gates Foundation, the Carlos Slim Foundation invests $25 million in a new bioscience complex in Mexico to help improve farmer productivity.

Slim is awarded the Medal of Honor by the International Shooting Sport Federation for his support of the sport.

COMPANIES AND INVESTMENTS

The following is a list of selected companies owned in whole or in part by Carlos Slim as well as other companies in which he has significant investments.

Conglomerate

Grupo Carso

Construction

Cementos Fortaleza
CICSA Ductos
CILSA
Elementia
IDEAL
PC Constructores
Servicios Integrales
Swecomex
Urvitec

Energy

Allis-Chalmers Energy
Gas Natural Fenosa
Tabasco Oil
YPF

Finance

Afore Inbursa
Banco Inbursa
BlackRock
CaixaBank
Casa de Bolsa Inversora Bursátil
Citigroup
Grupo Financiero Inbursa
Operadora Inbursa
Seguros Inbursa

Hotels

Calinda Beach Hotel Geneve
Grupo Hotelero Ostar
Ramada Gateway

Industrial Products and Supplies

CDM
Condumex Incorporated
Equiter
Grupo Condumex
Industrias IEM
Microm
Sinergia

Media

Grupo Prisa
Independent News & Media
Ora.Tv
Shazam
Stick Figure Productions
The New York Times Company

Medical Services

Grupo Star Médica

Mining

Minera Frisco

Real Estate

Inmuebles Carso

Retail

Dorian's
Grupo Sanborns
Mix-Up
Promotora Musical
Saks Fifth Avenue, Inc.
Sanborns Café
Sanborns Stores
Sears Mexico

Sports

Escudería Telmex
Grupo Pachuca
Real Oviedo

Telecommunications

América Móvil
Comcel
DLA
Embratel
Net Serviços
Porta
Sección Amarilla
Simple Mobile
Start Wireless Group
Telcel
Telekom Austria
Telmex

Telmex International
Tracfone

Transportation

Ferromex
Ferrosur

CITATIONS

Go Beyond Your Home

Gary Burnison, *No Fear of Failure: Real Stories of How Leaders Deal with Risk and Change*, 2011. San Francisco: Jossey-Bass. Kindle Edition.

Simplicity in Business

"Carlos Slim Interview." Academy of Achievement, December 2, 2007. http://www.achievement.org /autodoc/page/slioint-1.

The Benefit of Being Smaller

"President Bill Clinton, Frank Giustra and Carlos Slim Launch $20 Million Fund for Small- and Medium-sized Enterprises (SMEs) in Haiti." Clinton Foundation, June 17, 2010. http://www .clintonfoundation.org/main/news-and-media /press-releases-and-statements /press-release-president-bill-clinton-frank -giustra-and-carlos-slim-launch-20-mil.html.

Microsoft

Geri Smith, "Carlos Slim: 'The Key is the Internet.'" *Bloomberg Businessweek*, February 21, 2000. http:// www.businessweek.com/2000/00_08/b3669023.htm.

Focus on Operation

"Carlos Slim Interview." Academy of Achievement,
December 2, 2007. http://www.achievement.org
/autodoc/page/slioint-1.

His Father's Business Ventures

José Martinez, *Carlos Slim: The Richest Man in the
World*, 2013. Green Bay, Wisconsin: Titletown
Publishing. Kindle edition.

The Power of Excess

Gary Burnison, Eduardo Taylor, and Joel Kurtzman,
"Planting the Seeds of Wealth: An Interview with
Carlos Slim." *Korn/Ferry Briefings on Talent &
Leadership*, Fall 2010. http://www.kornferryinstitute
.com/briefings-magazine/fall-2010
/planting-seeds-wealth.

Learning from the Past

"Carlos Slim Interview." Academy of Achievement,
December 2, 2007. http://www.achievement.org
/autodoc/page/slioint-1.

Investing

"From Telecoms to Arts, Carlos Slim Promotes
Investment." *Agence France-Presse*, March 9, 2011.
http://www.google.com/hostednews/afp/article
/ALeqM5h1pcS8fpIwRfrNJPocSjVEI1NpMQ
?docId=CNG.5f4e1a89a5f643fa5f1a0508c3e346ae.ff1.

Money That Leaves

"Questions and Answers." 2007. http://www.carlosslim
.com/04_ing.html.

Reading a Company by the Numbers
"Interview with Carlos Slim." *Larry King Live*, December
3, 2011. http://transcripts.cnn.com
/TRANSCRIPTS/1012/03/lkl.01.html.

Risks
"Carlos Slim Interview." Academy of Achievement,
December 2, 2007. http://www.achievement.org
/autodoc/page/slioint-1.

His Role in the Telecommunications Market
Gustavo Camargo (translated by Daniel Cooke), "Slim
Faces the Giants." *Gazeta Mercantil*, March 13, 2000.

Share Prices
John Paul Rathbone and Adam Thomson, "Slim Shrugs
Off European Battering." *Financial Times*, February
25, 2013. http://www.ft.com/intl
/cms/s/0/29917698-7d02-11e2-adb6-00144feabdc0
.html#axzz2Mg2ON9G0.

Technology and Communications
Carlos Slim, Keynote Address at the National
Autonomous University of Mexico. Mexico City,
Mexico, June 21, 2010. http://www.carlosslim.com
/desde_slim_unammex_ing.html.

Telecommunications
Rogelio Estandía, (translator unknown) "It Is Possible
to Overcome the Crisis, but Not Only by Means of
Reform: Slim." *El Financiero*, October 19, 2009. http://
www.carlosslim.com/pdf/entrevista_financiero_ing
.pdf.

The *New York Times*

"Interview with Carlos Slim." *CNBC News*, October 30, 2008. https://www.youtube.com /watch?v=NK9bCWhfDHQ.

The Content

Lawrence Wright, "Slim's Time." *New Yorker*, June 1, 2009. http://www.newyorker.com /reporting/2009/06/01/090601fa_fact_ wright?currentPage=all.

Alliances

Geri Smith, "Carlos Slim: 'The Key is the Internet.'" *Bloomberg Businessweek*, February 21, 2000. http:// www.businessweek.com/2000/00_08/b3669023.htm.

Why His Company Is Bigger

Chris Hawley, "Carlos Slim Is the Richest Man You've Never Heard Of." *Arizona Republic*, May 30, 2007. http://www.azcentral.com/news/articles/2007/05/30 /20070530carlosslim0530.html.

They Will Run

Gary Burnison, Eduardo Taylor, and Joel Kurtzman, "Planting the Seeds of Wealth: An Interview with Carlos Slim." *Korn/Ferry Briefings on Talent & Leadership*, Fall 2010. http://www.kornferryinstitute .com/briefings-magazine/fall-2010 /planting-seeds-wealth.

Interconnections

James Blears, "Lunch with Slim." *Business Mexico*, volume 12 no. 8, August 2002.

Business Decisions

Geri Smith, Brian Grow, and John Cady, "The Sage of
Mexico City." *Bloomberg Businessweek*, March 28,
2005. http://www.businessweek.com
/stories/2005-03-27/the-sage-of-mexico-city.

His Business Goals

"Interview with Carlos Slim." *Larry King Live*, December
3, 2010. http://transcripts.cnn.com
/TRANSCRIPTS/1012/03/lkl.01.html.

Business Mortality

José Martinez, *Carlos Slim: The Richest Man in the
World*, 2013. Green Bay, Wisconsin: Titletown
Publishing. Kindle edition.

Acquisitions

Chris Hawley, "Carlos Slim Is the Richest Man You've
Never Heard Of." *Arizona Republic*, May 30, 2007.
http://www.azcentral.com/news/articles/2007/05/30
/20070530carlosslim0530.html.

Understanding How to Solve Problems

"Carlos Slim Interview." Academy of Achievement,
December 2, 2007. http://www.achievement.org
/autodoc/page/slioint-1.

Competition

"Questions and Answers." 2007. http://www.carlosslim
.com/17_ing.html.

Competition and Progress

José Martinez, *Carlos Slim: The Richest Man in the
World*, 2013. Green Bay, Wisconsin: Titletown
Publishing. Kindle edition.

Internal Competition

Gary Burnison, *No Fear of Failure: Real Stories of How Leaders Deal with Risk and Change*, 2011. San Francisco: Jossey-Bass. Kindle Edition.

Competitiveness

"Carlos Slim Promotes Education and Critical Thinking as a Means to Improve the Economy." American University of Beirut, March 18, 2010. http://www.aub.edu.lb/communications/media/Documents/Carlos-EN.pdf.

Executives versus Entrepreneurs

"Carlos Slim Interview." Academy of Achievement, December 2, 2007. http://www.achievement.org/autodoc/page/slioint-1.

They Will Have to Win It

Pilar Franco, "Finance-Mexico: Richest Latin American Sets Sights on US Market." *Inter Press Service*, February 10, 2000. http://www.ipsnews.net/2000/02/finance-mexico-richest-latin-american-sets-sights-on-us-market/.

Open to Competition

Elisabeth Malkin, "New Commitment to Charity by Mexican Phone Tycoon." *New York Times*, June 28, 2007. http://www.nytimes.com/2007/06/28/business/worldbusiness/28slim.html?pagewanted=all&_r=.

Fear of Competition

Eduardo Castillo, "Slim Denies He Has Monopoly on Mexico Telecom." *Yahoo! News*, February 1, 2012. http://news.yahoo.com/slim-denies-monopoly-mexico-telecom-012402325.html.

Getting into Crises

Reinhardt Krause, "Who's Mexico Gonna Call? Carlos Slim Helú." *Banderas News*, April 2007. http://banderasnews.com/0704/nz-carlosslimhelu.htm.

Crises Are Temporary

Noel Randewich, "World's Richest Man, Slim, a Born Wheeler-Dealer." *Reuters*, March 10, 2007. http://www.reuters.com/article/2010/03/10/slim-idUSN1014726920100310.

Opportunities

Miguel Jiménez and Amanda Mars (translated by Google), "All Crises Are Opportunities." *El País*, June 8, 2008. http://elpais.com/diario/2008/06/08/negocio/1212930865_850215.html.

Good or Bad Times

"World's Richest Man's Advice to Eurozone" (video). CNN, November 14, 2011. http://www.cnn.com/video/data/2.0/video/world/2011/11/14/ctw-carlos-slim.cnn.html.

Development for Business Reasons

Geri Smith, "Carlos Slim: 'The Key is the Internet.'" *Bloomberg Businessweek*, February 21, 2000. http://www.businessweek.com/2000/00_08/b3669023.htm.

Dividends

"Questions and Answers." 2007. http://www.carlosslim.com/15_ing.html.

Economic Cycles

"Carlos Slim Interview." Academy of Achievement,
    December 2, 2007. http://www.achievement.org
    /autodoc/page/slioint-1.

Globalization

"Questions and Answers." 2007. http://www.carlosslim
    .com/43_ing.html.

The Key Is the Internet

Geri Smith, "Carlos Slim: 'The Key is the Internet.'"
    Bloomberg Businessweek, February 21, 2000. http://
    www.businessweek.com/2000/00_08/b3669023.htm.

In Bad Shape

Gary Burnison, *No Fear of Failure: Real Stories of
    How Leaders Deal with Risk and Change*, 2011. San
    Francisco: Jossey-Bass. Kindle Edition.

Investment Philosophy

Lawrence Wright, "Slim's Time." *New Yorker*, June 1,
    2009. http://www.newyorker.com
    /reporting/2009/06/01/090601fa_fact_
    wright?currentPage=all.

Investing Excessively

"Carlos Slim Interview." Academy of Achievement,
    December 2, 2007. http://www.achievement.org
    /autodoc/page/slioint-1.

Investing in Developed versus Emerging Markets

John Rathbone and Adam Thomson, "Carlos Slim Eyes
    Latin America For Growth." *Financial Times*, June 12,
    2011. http://www.ft.com/intl/cms/s/0
    /07e4dcd4-9518-11e0-a648-00144feab49a
    .html#axzz2Hxene9Z3.

Investing in Mexico

"A Conversation with Carlos Slim." *Leaders*, October–
December 2012. http://www.leadersmag.com
/issues/2012.4_Oct/ROB
/LEADERS-Carlos-Slim-Helu-Grupo-Carso.html.

Investing in Latin America

John Rathbone and Adam Thomson, "Carlos Slim Eyes
Latin America For Growth." *Financial Times*, June 12,
2011. http://www.ft.com/intl/cms/s/0
/07e4dcd4-9518-11e0-a648-00144feab49a
.html#axzz2Hxene9Z3.

Clear, Attainable Targets

Jonathan Kandell, "Slim City." *Institutional Investor*,
June 1, 2003. http://www.institutionalinvestor.com
/Popups/PrintArticle.aspx?ArticleID=1026893.

Investors versus Entrepreneurs

"A Conversation with Carlos Slim." *Leaders*, October–
December 2012. http://www.leadersmag.com
/issues/2012.4_Oct/ROB
/LEADERS-Carlos-Slim-Helu-Grupo-Carso.html.

US Investments in Mexico

Gary Burnison, Eduardo Taylor, and Joel Kurtzman,
"Planting the Seeds of Wealth: An Interview with
Carlos Slim." *Korn/Ferry Briefings on Talent &
Leadership*, Fall 2010. http://www.kornferryinstitute
.com/briefings-magazine/fall-2010
/planting-seeds-wealth.

Avoid Large Mistakes

Jonathan Kandell, "Slim City." *Institutional Investor*,
    June 1, 2003. http://www.institutionalinvestor.com
    /Popups/PrintArticle.aspx?ArticleID=1026893.

Old-Style Business

Geri Smith, "Carlos Slim: 'The Key is the Internet.'"
    Bloomberg Businessweek, February 21, 2000. http://
    www.businessweek.com/2000/00_08/b3669023.htm.

How He Has Developed as a Businessman over Time

Gary Burnison, Eduardo Taylor, and Joel Kurtzman,
    "Planting the Seeds of Wealth: An Interview with
    Carlos Slim." *Korn/Ferry Briefings on Talent &
    Leadership*, Fall 2010. http://www.kornferryinstitute
    .com/briefings-magazine/fall-2010
    /planting-seeds-wealth.

Giving People a Sense of Purpose

Gary Burnison, Eduardo Taylor, and Joel Kurtzman,
    "Planting the Seeds of Wealth: An Interview with
    Carlos Slim." *Korn/Ferry Briefings on Talent &
    Leadership*, Fall 2010. http://www.kornferryinstitute
    .com/briefings-magazine/fall-2010
    /planting-seeds-wealth.

Mistakes

Miguel Jiménéz and Amanda Mars (translated by
    Google), "All Crises Are Opportunities." *El País*, June
    8, 2008. http://elpais.com/diario/2008/06/08
    /negocio/1212930865_850215.html.

The Worst Mistake

"Carlos Slim Interviewed at the WTTC Americas Summit." May 17, 2012. http://www.youtube.com /watch?v=ATzcv324kbY

Emotional Needs

Gary Burnison, Eduardo Taylor, and Joel Kurtzman, "Planting the Seeds of Wealth: An Interview with Carlos Slim." *Korn/Ferry Briefings on Talent & Leadership*, Fall 2010. http://www.kornferryinstitute .com/briefings-magazine/fall-2010 /planting-seeds-wealth.

Developing Leaders from the Inside

Gary Burnison, Eduardo Taylor, and Joel Kurtzman, "Planting the Seeds of Wealth: An Interview with Carlos Slim." *Korn/Ferry Briefings on Talent & Leadership*, Fall 2010. http://www.kornferryinstitute .com/briefings-magazine/fall-2010 /planting-seeds-wealth.

Leadership Attributes

Carlos Slim, Keynote Address at the First International Congress of Miraflores College. Valdivia, Chile, February 12, 2011. http://www.carlosslim.com/desde_ slim_miraflores_ing.html.

Management Layers

Geri Smith, "Carlos Slim: 'The Key is the Internet.'" *Bloomberg Businessweek*, February 21, 2000. http:// www.businessweek.com/2000/00_08/b3669023.htm.

Organizational Culture

Gary Burnison, Eduardo Taylor, and Joel Kurtzman,
"Planting the Seeds of Wealth: An Interview with
Carlos Slim." *Korn/Ferry Briefings on Talent &
Leadership*, Fall 2010. http://www.kornferryinstitute
.com/briefings-magazine/fall-2010
/planting-seeds-wealth.

Teamwork

"Carlos Slim Interview." Academy of Achievement,
December 2, 2007. http://www.achievement.org
/autodoc/page/slioint-1.

Creating

Gary Burnison, Eduardo Taylor, and Joel Kurtzman,
"Planting the Seeds of Wealth: An Interview with
Carlos Slim." *Korn/Ferry Briefings on Talent &
Leadership*, Fall 2010. http://www.kornferryinstitute
.com/briefings-magazine/fall-2010
/planting-seeds-wealth.

Developing Human Capital

Gary Burnison, Eduardo Taylor, and Joel Kurtzman,
"Planting the Seeds of Wealth: An Interview with
Carlos Slim." *Korn/Ferry Briefings on Talent &
Leadership*, Fall 2010. http://www.kornferryinstitute
.com/briefings-magazine/fall-2010
/planting-seeds-wealth.

Employees

Gary Burnison, Eduardo Taylor, and Joel Kurtzman, "Planting the Seeds of Wealth: An Interview with Carlos Slim." *Korn/Ferry Briefings on Talent & Leadership*, Fall 2010. http://www.kornferryinstitute.com/briefings-magazine/fall-2010/planting-seeds-wealth.

Achievements

Gary Burnison, *No Fear of Failure: Real Stories of How Leaders Deal with Risk and Change*, 2011. San Francisco: Jossey-Bass. Kindle Edition.

Facing Our Problems

"Carlos Slim Promotes Education and Critical Thinking as a Means to Improve the Economy." American University of Beirut, March 18, 2010. http://www.aub.edu.lb/communications/media/Documents/Carlos-EN.pdf.

Founders versus CEOs

Gary Burnison, Eduardo Taylor, and Joel Kurtzman, "Planting the Seeds of Wealth: An Interview with Carlos Slim." *Korn/Ferry Briefings on Talent & Leadership*, Fall 2010. http://www.kornferryinstitute.com/briefings-magazine/fall-2010/planting-seeds-wealth.

How to Identify Great Leaders

Gary Burnison, Eduardo Taylor, and Joel Kurtzman, "Planting the Seeds of Wealth: An Interview with Carlos Slim." *Korn/Ferry Briefings on Talent & Leadership*, Fall 2010. http://www.kornferryinstitute.com/briefings-magazine/fall-2010/planting-seeds-wealth.

Being Rich

Adam Thomson, "Interview with Carlos Slim." *Financial Times*, September 27, 2007. http://www.ft.com /cms/s/0/86e041d8-6d24-11dc-ab19-0000779fd2ac .html#axzz2HyTGeslk.

What Keeps Him Awake at Night

"World's Richest Man's Advice to Eurozone" (video). CNN, added November 14, 2011. http://www.cnn.com/video /data/2.0/video/world/2011/11/14/ctw-carlos-slim.cnn .html.

Accept Them, Correct Them, and Forget Them

"Carlos Slim Promotes Education and Critical Thinking as a Means to Improve the Economy." American University of Beirut, March 18, 2010. http://www.aub.edu.lb /communications/media/Documents/Carlos-EN.pdf.

Optimism

"Questions and Answers." 2007. http://www.carlosslim .com/04_ing.html.

Pessismism

Carlos Slim, Commencement Speech at George Washington University (video). Washington, DC, May 19, 2012. http://www.youtube.com/v /e5ddwLTUhf0?version=3&hl=en_US.

Money

Gary Burnison, Eduardo Taylor, and Joel Kurtzman, "Planting the Seeds of Wealth: An Interview with Carlos Slim." *Korn/Ferry Briefings on Talent & Leadership*, Fall 2010. http://www.kornferryinstitute.com /briefings-magazine/fall-2010/planting-seeds-wealth.

Negative Feelings and Emotions

"Letter to Young People." June 1994. http://www
.carlosslim.com/carta_ing.html.

The Numbers

Lawrence Wright, "Slim's Time." *New Yorker*, June 1,
2009. http://www.newyorker.com
/reporting/2009/06/01/090601fa_fact_
wright?currentPage=all.

Words versus Numbers

Chris Hawley, "Carlos Slim Is the Richest Man You've
Never Heard Of." *Arizona Republic*, May 30, 2007.
http://www.azcentral.com/news/articles/2007/05/30
/20070530carlosslim0530.html.

Time Management

"Carlos Slim Interview." Academy of Achievement,
December 2, 2007. http://www.achievement.org
/autodoc/page/slioint-1.

Vocations

José Martinez, *Carlos Slim: The Richest Man in the
World*, 2013. Green Bay, Wisconsin: Titletown
Publishing. Kindle edition.

Wealth Distribution

Gary Burnison, Eduardo Taylor, and Joel Kurtzman,
"Planting the Seeds of Wealth: An Interview with
Carlos Slim." *Korn/Ferry Briefings on Talent &
Leadership*, Fall 2010. http://www.kornferryinstitute
.com/briefings-magazine/fall-2010
/planting-seeds-wealth.

Wealth Is Like an Orchard

Heidi Blake, "Carlos Slim: Profile of the World's Richest Man." *Telegraph*, March 11, 2010. http://www .telegraph.co.uk/finance/7419211 /Carlos-Slim-profile-of-the-worlds-richest-man.html.

What It Means to Him to Be the Richest Person in the World

"Interview with Carlos Slim" (video). *ABC News*, October 8, 2007. http://www.youtube.com /watch?v=oREE2OeyoQU.

Water off a Duck's Back

"Mexico Leads *Fortune* Rich List." *BBC News*, August 7, 2007. http://news.bbc.co.uk/2/hi/business/6934418 .stm.

Why He Doesn't Live in a Bigger House

Adam Thomson, "Interview with Carlos Slim." *Financial Times*, September 27, 2007. http://www.ft.com /cms/s/0/86e041d8-6d24-11dc-ab19-0000779fd2ac .html#axzz2HyTGeslk.

Why He Won't Retire

Julia Finch and Jo Tuckman, "Profile: Carlos Slim." *Guardian*, July 6, 2007. http://www.guardian.co.uk /business/2007/jul/06/4.

Words He Lives By

Gary Burnison, Eduardo Taylor, and Joel Kurtzman, "Planting the Seeds of Wealth: An Interview with Carlos Slim." *Korn/Ferry Briefings on Talent & Leadership*, Fall 2010. http://www.kornferryinstitute .com/briefings-magazine/fall-2010 /planting-seeds-wealth.

Work

Gary Burnison, *No Fear of Failure: Real Stories of How Leaders Deal with Risk and Change*, 2011. San Francisco: Jossey-Bass. Kindle Edition.

Being Like Warren Buffett

Geri Smith, "Carlos Slim: 'The Key is the Internet.'" *Bloomberg Businessweek*, February 21, 2000. http://www.businessweek.com/2000/00_08/b3669023.htm.

The New York Yankees

Lloyd Grove, "Carlos Slim Fixes the Economy." *Daily Beast*, September 27, 2011. http://www.thedailybeast.com/articles/2011/09/27/carlos-slim-on-how-to-fix-the-u-s-economy.html.

Computers

Geri Smith, "Carlos Slim: 'The Key is the Internet.'" *Bloomberg Businessweek*, February 21, 2000. http://www.businessweek.com/2000/00_08/b3669023.htm.

Paper Man

Simon Atkinson, "Profile: Carlos Slim." *BBC News*, July 4, 2007. http://news.bbc.co.uk/2/hi/business/6269064.stm.

His Critics

Lawrence Wright, "Slim's Time." *New Yorker*, June 1, 2009. http://www.newyorker.com/reporting/2009/06/01/090601fa_fact_wright?currentPage=all.

Public Opinion

Stephanie Mehta, "Carlos Slim: The Richest Man in the World." *Fortune*, August 20, 2007. http://money.cnn.com/2007/08/03/news/international/carlosslim.fortune.

Early Start

"Interview with Carlos Slim." *Larry King Live*, December 3, 2010. http://transcripts.cnn.com/TRANSCRIPTS/1012/03/lkl.01.html.

Family Business

Jonathan Kandell, "Slim City." *Institutional Investor*, June 1, 2003. http://www.institutionalinvestor.com/Popups/PrintArticle.aspx?ArticleID=1026893.

Find the Job for Their Strengths

José Martinez, *Carlos Slim: The Richest Man in the World*, 2013. Green Bay, Wisconsin: Titletown Publishing. Kindle edition.

His Biggest Influence

Gary Burnison, Eduardo Taylor, and Joel Kurtzman, "Planting the Seeds of Wealth: An Interview with Carlos Slim." *Korn/Ferry Briefings on Talent & Leadership*, Fall 2010. http://www.kornferryinstitute.com/briefings-magazine/fall-2010/planting-seeds-wealth.

Fear and Guilt

Carlos Slim, Commencement Speech at George Washington University (video). Washington, DC, May 19, 2012. http://www.youtube.com/v/e5ddwLTUhfo?version=3&hl=en_US.

Follow Your Conscience

"Letter to Young People." June 1994. http://www
.carlosslim.com/carta_ing.html.

Fortitude and Emotional Balance

Carlos Slim, Commencement Speech at George
Washington University (video). Washington, DC,
May 19, 2012. http://www.youtube.com/v
/e5ddwLTUhfo?version=3&hl=en_US.

Freedom

"Carlos Slim Interview." Academy of Achievement,
December 2, 2007. http://www.achievement.org
/autodoc/page/slioint-1.

Happiness

Carlos Slim, Commencement Speech at George
Washington University (video). Washington, DC,
May 19, 2012. http://www.youtube.com/v
/e5ddwLTUhfo?version=3&hl=en_US.

Money Can't Buy Happiness

"Interview with Carlos Slim." *Larry King Live*, December
3, 2010. http://transcripts.cnn.com
/TRANSCRIPTS/1012/03/lkl.01.html.

How He Spends His Time

Geri Smith, "Carlos Slim: 'The Key is the Internet.'"
Bloomberg Businessweek, February 21, 2000. http://
www.businessweek.com/2000/00_08/b3669023.htm.

Company Analysis

Reuters and Thais Costa (translated by James Bruce),
"Telmex Confirms TIM Interest in Latin America."
Gazeta Mercantil, November 23, 2004.

His Job

Lawrence Wright, "Slim's Time." *New Yorker*, June 1,
    2009. http://www.newyorker.com
    /reporting/2009/06/01/090601fa_fact_
    wright?currentPage=all.

How He Thinks of Himself

Gary Burnison, Eduardo Taylor, and Joel Kurtzman,
    "Planting the Seeds of Wealth: An Interview with
    Carlos Slim." *Korn/Ferry Briefings on Talent &
    Leadership*, Fall 2010. http://www.kornferryinstitute
    .com/briefings-magazine/fall-2010
    /planting-seeds-wealth.

Work Is an Emotional Need

"Carlos Slim Interview." Academy of Achievement,
    December 2, 2007. http://www.achievement.org
    /autodoc/page/slioint-1.

Work–Life Balance

"Carlos Slim Interview." Academy of Achievement,
    December 2, 2007. http://www.achievement.org
    /autodoc/page/slioint-1.

Family Life Is Crucial

Carlos Slim, Keynote Address at the First International
    Congress of Miraflores College. Valdivia, Chile,
    February 12, 2011. http://www.carlosslim.com/desde_
    slim_miraflores_ing.html.

Worrying about Others' Opinions

"The Richest People You've Never Heard Of." *Forbes*,
    June 1, 2007. http://www.forbes
    .com/2007/06/01/billionaires-helu-gates-buffett-biz_
    cx_0601unknownrich.html.

Needing Others to Say Good Things
"Carlos Slim Interview." Academy of Achievement, December 2, 2007. http://www.achievement.org /autodoc/page/slioint-1.

One's Own Sense of Accomplishment
Cyntia Diaz, "Carlos Slim Ranks as World's Richest Person For Second Year." *Reuters*, March 9, 2011. http://www.reuters.com/article/2011/03/10 /us-billionaires-slim-idUSTRE72900O20110310.

Success
"Letter to Young People." June 1994. http://www .carlosslim.com/desde_ing.html#carta.

Success Is Your Life
"Carlos Slim Interview." Academy of Achievement, December 2, 2007. http://www.achievement.org /autodoc/page/slioint-1.

How He'll Be Remembered
José Martinez, *Carlos Slim: The Richest Man in the World*, 2013. Green Bay, Wisconsin: Titletown Publishing. Kindle edition.

A Positive Influence
"Letter to Young People." June 1994. http://www .carlosslim.com/desde_ing.html#carta.

Lessons From His Father
Gary Burnison, *No Fear of Failure: Real Stories of How Leaders Deal with Risk and Change*, 2011. San Francisco: Jossey-Bass. Kindle Edition.

We Can Only Do Things While Alive

"Questions and Answers." 2007. http://www.carlosslim
.com/04_ing.html.

Living

Carlos Slim, Commencement Speech at George
Washington University (video). Washington, DC,
May 19, 2012. http://www.youtube.com/v
/e5ddwLTUhfo?version=3&hl=en_US.

Leaving Better Children for His World

Stephanie Mehta, "Carlos Slim: The Richest Man in the
World." *Fortune*, August 20, 2007. http://money
.cnn.com/2007/08/03/news/international/carlosslim
.fortune.

Leaving Children a Commitment

Reinhardt Krause, "Who's Mexico Gonna Call? Carlos
Slim Helú." *Banderas News*, April 2007. http://
banderasnews.com/0704/nz-carlosslimhelu.htm.

Leaving Children Money

"Questions and Answers." 2007. http://www.carlosslim
.com/20_ing.html.

His Legacy

Chris Hawley, "Carlos Slim Is the Richest Man You've
Never Heard Of." *Arizona Republic*, May 30, 2007.
http://www.azcentral.com/news/articles/2007/05/30
/20070530carlosslim0530.html.

Learning From Personal Crises

Lawrence Wright, "Slim's Time." *New Yorker*, June 1, 2009. http://www.newyorker.com /reporting/2009/06/01/090601fa_fact_ wright?currentPage=all.

Life

"Letter to Young People." June 1994. http://www .carlosslim.com/carta_ing.html.

What's Worthwhile Has No Price

Carlos Slim, Commencement Speech at George Washington University (video). Washington, DC, May 19, 2012. http://www.youtube.com/v /e5ddwLTUhf0?version=3&hl=en_US.

Enjoy Life

"Letter to Young People." June 1994. http://www .carlosslim.com/carta_ing.html.

Living Modestly

Kerry Dolan, "The World According to Slim." *Forbes*, March 7, 2012. http://www.forbes .com/forbes/2012/0326 /billionaires-12-feature-telecommunications-mexico -world-according-carlos-slim.html.

A Big Place

"Interview with Carlos Slim." *Larry King Live*, December 3, 2010. http://transcripts.cnn.com /TRANSCRIPTS/1012/03/lkl.01.html.

Luck

"Interview with Carlos Slim" (video). George
    Washington University Global Forum, New York,
    October 29, 2010. http://www.youtube.com
    /watch?v=DmwBgNakYYQ.

Lying

"Carlos Slim Promotes Education and Critical Thinking
    as a Means to Improve the Economy." American
    University of Beirut, March 18, 2010. http://www
    .aub.edu.lb/communications/media/Documents
    /Carlos-EN.pdf.

A Lie Repeated

Chris Hawley, "Carlos Slim is the Richest Man You've
    Never Heard Of." *Arizona Republic*, May 30, 2007.
    http://www.azcentral.com/news/articles/2007/05/30
    /20070530carlosslim0530.html.

His Philanthropic Efforts

Adam Thomson, "Interview with Carlos Slim." *Financial
    Times*, September 27, 2007. http://www.ft.com/intl
    /cms/s/0/86e041d8-6d24-11dc-ab19-0000779fd2ac
    .html#axzz2Hxene9Z3.

We Don't Give Money

"A Conversation with Larry King and Carlos Slim"
    (video). Milken Institute Global Forum, Los Angeles,
    California, April 29, 2013. http://www
    .milkeninstitute.org/events/gcprogram.taf?function=
    detail&EvID=4014&eventid=GC13%27.

Not a Problem of Money

Helen Coster, "Slim's Chance to Change His Legacy."
 Forbes, March 9, 2007. http://www.msnbc.msn.com
 /id/17506956/ns/business-forbes_com/t
 /slims-chance-change-his-legacy.

Philanthropy

"A Conversation with Carlos Slim." *Leaders*, October–
 December 2012. http://www.leadersmag.com
 /issues/2012.4_Oct/ROB/LEADERS-Carlos-Slim
 -Helu-Grupo-Carso.html.

To Do and to Solve

"Questions and Answers." 2007. http://www.carlosslim
 .com/38_ing.html.

Social Responsibility of Business Leaders

Geri Smith, "Carlos Slim: 'The Key is the Internet.'"
 Bloomberg Businessweek, February 21, 2000. http://
 www.businessweek.com/2000/00_08/b3669023.htm.

Wealth as a Social Responsibility

Mark Stevenson, "Latin America's Richest Man Calls
 For Reducing Poverty." *Highbeam*, September 7, 2005.
 http://www.highbeam.com/doc/1P1-112912900.html.

Produce Wealth for Society

"Carlos Slim Interview." Academy of Achievement,
 December 2, 2007. http://www.achievement.org
 /autodoc/page/slioint-1.

Warren Buffett's Philanthropic Efforts

Mark Stevenson, "Mexican Billionaire: Business, not Santa, Solves Ills." *Pittsburgh Post-Gazette*, March 14, 2007. http://www.post-gazette.com /businessnews/2007/03/14 /Mexican-billionaire-Business-not-Santa-solves-ills /stories/200703140199.

Bill Gates's Philanthropic Efforts

Mark Stevenson, "Mexican Billionaire: Business, not Santa, Solves Ills." *Pittsburgh Post-Gazette*, March 14, 2007. http://www.post-gazette.com/stories/business /news/mexican-billionaire-business-not-santa-solves -ills-476254.

The Problem of Poverty

"Profile: Carlos Slim." *BBC News*, March 10, 2010. http:// news.bbc.co.uk/2/hi/8560812.stm.

Funding Charities

Jennifer Dauble, "CNBC Exclusive: CNBC Transcript: CNBC's Michelle Caruso-Cabrera Sits Down With Carlos Slim, The World's Wealthiest Man, Today On CNBC." *CNBC*, January 20, 2011. http://www.cnbc. com/id/40969362 /cnbc_exclusive_cnbc_transcript_cnbc039s_%20 michelle_carusocabrera_sits_down_with_carlos_ slim_the_world039s_wealthiest_man_today_on_cnbc.

Businesspeople as Social-Problem Solvers

"A Conversation with Carlos Slim." *Leaders*, October–December 2012. http://www.leadersmag.com /issues/2012.4_Oct/ROB /LEADERS-Carlos-Slim-Helu-Grupo-Carso.html.

Our Knowledge and Experience

"A Conversation with Carlos Slim." *Leaders*, October–December 2012. http://www.leadersmag.com/issues/2012.4_Oct/ROB/LEADERS-Carlos-Slim-Helu-Grupo-Carso.html.

Social Challenges

Adam Thomson, "Interview with Carlos Slim." *Financial Times*, September 27, 2007. http://www.ft.com/intl/cms/s/0/86e041d8-6d24-11dc-ab19-0000779fd2ac.html#axzz2Hxene9Z3.

His Challenge in Life

"A Conversation with Carlos Slim." *Leaders*, October–December 2012. http://www.leadersmag.com/issues/2012.4_Oct/ROB/LEADERS-Carlos-Slim-Helu-Grupo-Carso.html.

Working Together

"Questions and Answers." 2007. http://www.carlosslim.com/04_ing.html

Charity

Anne Hyland with Jenny Wiggins, "Donations Don't Work: Slim." *Australian Financial Review*, September 30, 2010. http://www.afr.com/p/business/companies/donations_don_work_slim_x00eekz2ln5HvYAFDSHWWM.

Poverty

"Interview with Carlos Slim" (video). George Washington University Global Forum, New York, October 29, 2010. http://www.youtube.com/watch?v=DmwBgNakYYQ.

Digital University

Lloyd Grove, "Carlos Slim Fixes the Economy." *Daily Beast*, September 27, 2011. http://www.thedailybeast .com/articles/2011/09/27 /carlos-slim-on-how-to-fix-the-u-s-economy.html.

Education

"A Conversation with Carlos Slim." *Leaders*, October–December 2012. http://www.leadersmag.com /issues/2012.4_Oct/ROB /LEADERS-Carlos-Slim-Helu-Grupo-Carso.html.

Teach Creative Thinking

"Carlos Slim Promotes Education and Critical Thinking as a Means to Improve the Economy." American University of Beirut, March 18, 2010. http://www .aub.edu.lb/communications/media/Documents /Carlos-EN.pdf.

Domestication

"Carlos Slim Interview." Academy of Achievement, December 2, 2007. http://www.achievement.org /autodoc/page/slioint-1.

Understanding the World

Gary Burnison, Eduardo Taylor, and Joel Kurtzman, "Planting the Seeds of Wealth: An Interview with Carlos Slim." *Korn/Ferry Briefings on Talent & Leadership*, Fall 2010. http://www.kornferryinstitute .com/briefings-magazine/fall-2010 /planting-seeds-wealth.

Fighting Poverty

"Questions and Answers." 2007. http://www.carlosslim
.com/43_ing.html.

Poverty as an Obstacle

"Carlos Slim Interview." Academy of Achievement,
December 2, 2007. http://www.achievement.org
/autodoc/page/slioint-1.

The Answer is Jobs

John Rathbone and Adam Thomson, "World's Richest
Man Stays Down to Earth." *Financial Times*, June 12,
2011. http://www.ft.com/intl/cms/s/0
/d854c950-93a7-11e0-922e-00144feab49a
.html#axzz2Hxene9Z3.

The Best Investment

Chiara Reid, "Carlos Slim: I Am Not a Monopoliser."
Euronews, October 26, 2011. http://www.euronews
.com/2011/10/26/carlos-slim-i-am-not-a-monopoliser/.

Fighting Poverty—but Not with Charity

Jennifer Dauble, "CNBC Exclusive: CNBC Transcript:
CNBC's Michelle Caruso-Cabrera Sits Down With
Carlos Slim, The World's Wealthiest Man, Today On
CNBC." *CNBC*, January 20, 2011. http://www.cnbc
.com/id/40969362/cnbc_exclusive_cnbc_transcript_
cnbc039s_%20michelle_carusocabrera_sits_down_
with_carlos_slim_the_world039s_wealthiest_man_
today_on_cnbc.

Support, Not Money

Kerry Dolan, "The World According to Slim." *Forbes*,
March 7, 2012. http://www.forbes
.com/forbes/2012/0326
/billionaires-12-feature-telecommunications
-mexico-world-according-carlos-slim.html.

Doing Instead of Giving

Chris Aspen, "Mexico's Slim Nears Gates on World-
Richest List." *Reuters*, April 12, 2007. http://www
.reuters.com/article/2007/04/12
/us-mexico-slim-idUSN1229571820070412.

Santa Claus

Mark Stevenson, "Mexican Billionaire: Business, not
Santa, Solves Ills." *Pittsburgh Post-Gazette*, March 14,
2007. http://www.post-gazette.com
/businessnews/2007/03/14
/Mexican-billionaire-Business-not-Santa-solves-ills
/stories/200703140199.

Fighting Poverty through Partnerships

Gary Burnison, *No Fear of Failure: Real Stories of
How Leaders Deal with Risk and Change*, 2011. San
Francisco: Jossey-Bass. Kindle Edition.

Fighting Poverty with Education and Jobs

Elisabeth Malkin, "New Commitment to Charity by
Mexican Phone Tycoon." *New York Times*, June 28,
2007. http://www.nytimes.com/2007/06/28/business
/worldbusiness/28slim.html?pagewanted=all.

Dignity

"President Bill Clinton, Frank Giustra and Carlos Slim Launch $20 Million Fund for Small- and Medium-sized Enterprises (SMEs) in Haiti." Clinton Foundation, June 17, 2010. http://www .clintonfoundation.org/main/news-and-media /press-releases-and-statements/press-release -president-bill-clinton-frank-giustra-and-carlos-slim -launch-20-mil.html.

Improving the Economy via Education and Training

"A Conversation with Carlos Slim." *Leaders*, October– December 2012. http://www.leadersmag.com /issues/2012.4_Oct/ROB /LEADERS-Carlos-Slim-Helu-Grupo-Carso.html.

Giving and Receiving

"Letter to Young People." June 1994. http://www .carlosslim.com/carta_ing.html.

Universal Access to the Internet

"Interview with Carlos Slim" (video). *CNBC News*, November 16, 2009. http://video.cnbc.com /gallery/?video=1333032769.

Business People versus Politicians

Kerry Dolan, "The World According to Slim." *Forbes*, March 7, 2012. http://www.forbes .com/forbes/2012/0326 /billionaires-12-feature-telecommunications -mexico-world-according-carlos-slim.html.

$1

"A Conversation with Larry King and Carlos Slim"
(video). Milken Institute Global Forum, Los Angeles,
California, April 29, 2013. http://www
.milkeninstitute.org/events/gcprogram.taf?function=
detail&EvID=4014&eventid=GC13%27.

Democracy

"Questions and Answers." 2007. http://www.carlosslim
.com/39_ing.html.

Economic Recovery

Crayton Harrison and Lindsey Arent, "Carlos Slim Says
Jobs, Construction Are Key to Growth." *Bloomberg*,
November 17, 2009. http://www.bloomberg.com/apps
/news?pid=newsarchive&sid=aZ26byqelOAU.

Economic Stability

Mark Stevenson, "Latin America's Richest Man Calls For
Reducing Poverty." *Free Republic*, September 7, 2005.
http://www.freerepublic.com/focus/f-news/1479656
/posts.

Public and Private Investment

"Carlos Slim Interview." Academy of Achievement,
December 2, 2007. http://www.achievement.org
/autodoc/page/slioint-1.

Free Trade

"Questions and Answers." 2007. http://www.carlosslim
.com/46_ing.html.

Immigrants

"Carlos Slim Interview." Academy of Achievement, December 2, 2007. http://www.achievement.org /autodoc/page/slioint-1.

Mexico's Drug War

Lloyd Grove, "Carlos Slim Fixes the Economy." *Daily Beast*, September 27, 2011. http://www.thedailybeast .com/articles/2011/09/27 /carlos-slim-on-how-to-fix-the-u-s-economy.html.

Mexico's Federal Competition Commission

Alexander Hanrath, "Kill the Ref: A Competition Watchdog Struggles to Grow Teeth in a Changing Mexico." *Latin Trade*, November, 2002. http://www .thefreelibrary.com/Kill+the+ref%3A+a+competition+ watchdog+struggles+to+grow+teeth+in+ a...-a094764266.

Political Ambitions

"Questions and Answers." 2007. http://www.carlosslim .com/50_ing.html.

Political Leanings

José Martinez, *Carlos Slim: The Richest Man in the World*, 2013. Green Bay, Wisconsin: Titletown Publishing. Kindle edition.

Political Leaders

Kerry Dolan, "The World According to Slim." *Forbes*, March 7, 2012. http://www.forbes .com/forbes/2012/0326 /billionaires-12-feature-telecommunications-mexico -world-according-carlos-slim.html.

46

RLD'S RICHEST MAN

President Obama's Buffett Rule

Lloyd Grove, "Carlos Slim Fixes the Economy." *Daily Beast*, September 27, 2011. http://www.thedailybeast.com/articles/2011/09/27/carlos-slim-on-how-to-fix-the-u-s-economy.html.

Pride

Miguel Jiménez and Amanda Mars (translated by Google), "All Crises Are Opportunities." *El País*, June 8, 2008. http://elpais.com/diario/2008/06/08/negocio/1212930865_850215.html.

Prosperity

Gary Burnison, Eduardo Taylor, and Joel Kurtzman, "Planting the Seeds of Wealth: An Interview with Carlos Slim." *Korn/Ferry Briefings on Talent & Leadership*, Fall 2010. http://www.kornferryinstitute.com/briefings-magazine/fall-2010/planting-seeds-wealth.

His Relationship with Government Officials in Latin America

Amy Guthrie, "Billionaire Carlos Slim Predicts Better Days Ahead for Mexico." *Wall Street Journal*, October 8, 2003. http://online.wsj.com/news/articles/SB106565404478988800.

Known by the Public

"Questions and Answers." 2007. http://www.carlosslim.com/40_ing.html.

Retirement Age

Harriet Alexander, "Carlos Slim: Developed Nations
Face Chronic Problem From Ageing Population."
Telegraph, February 19, 2011. http://www.telegraph
.co.uk/finance/globalbusiness/8335710
/Carlos-Slim-Developed-nations-face-chronic
-problem-from-ageing-population.html.

Company Size

"Rwanda: Make Broadband Access a Global Priority—
Kagame." *All Africa*, April 3, 2012. http://allafrica
.com/stories/201204040053.html?page=2.

Where the Employment Is

Lloyd Grove, "Carlos Slim Fixes the Economy." *Daily
Beast*, September 27, 2011. http://www.thedailybeast
.com/articles/2011/09/27
/carlos-slim-on-how-to-fix-the-u-s-economy.html.

Solving the European Economic Crisis

Philip Inman, "Sort Out Eurozone Crisis, World Tells
Europe's Leaders." *Guardian*, October 17, 2012. http://
www.guardian.co.uk/world/2012/oct/17
/eurozone-crisis-europe-world-leaders.

Adjustments to the Welfare State

Salvador Camarena, "'It is time to make some
adjustments to this welfare state': Mexican Magnate
Carlos Slim Gives His Views on Europe's Crisis." *El
País*, October 21, 2012. http://elpais.com
/elpais/2012/10/21/inenglish/1350822715_643244.html.

Europe's Assets

"Slim: Party Should Begin at the Airport." *Mexico Today*,
    May 30, 2012. http://mexicotoday.org
    /economy/mexican-businessman-carlos-slim-travel
    -tourism-industry-no-more-%E2%80%9Cthink
    -tank%E2%80%9D-mentality-and-m.

Solving the US Economic Crisis

Lloyd Grove, "Carlos Slim Fixes the Economy." *Daily
    Beast,* September 27, 2011. http://www.thedailybeast
    .com/articles/2011/09/27
    /carlos-slim-on-how-to-fix-the-u-s-economy.html.

The Public Sector

Robert Frank, "World's Richest Man Attacks Wall Street
    Bailouts." *Wall Street Journal*, October 25, 2011.
    http://blogs.wsj.com/wealth/2011/10/25
    /worlds-richest-man-attacks-wall-street-bailouts.

Modern Marshall Plan

Geri Smith, "Carlos Slim: 'The Key is the Internet.'"
    Bloomberg Businessweek, February 21, 2000. http://
    www.businessweek.com/2000/00_08/b3669023.htm.

Support the System

"Interview with Carlos Slim." *CNBC News*, October 30,
    2008. https://www.youtube.com
    /watch?v=NK9bCWhfDHQ.

Developing Latin America

Adam Thomson, "Interview with Carlos Slim." *Financial
    Times*, September 27, 2007. http://www.ft.com/intl
    /cms/s/0/86e041d8-6d24-11dc-ab19-0000779fd2ac
    .html#axzz2Hxene9Z3.

ABOUT THE EDITOR

Tanni Haas, PhD, is a full professor in the Department of Speech Communication Arts & Sciences at the City University of New York—Brooklyn College, where he teaches courses on business communication and other topics. He is the author of two books, *Making It in the Political Blogosphere: The World's Top Political Bloggers Share the Secrets to Success* and *The Pursuit of Public Journalism: Theory, Practice, and Criticism* (which has been translated into Chinese and Korean), as well as more than three dozen scholarly journal articles and book chapters.